10 THINGS YOU GOTTA KNOW

About

Your First Year of College

Nikki Moustaki

SPARK
COLLEGE

AN IMPRINT OF SPARK PUBLISHING

WWW.SPARKCOLLEGE.COM

Steven, I thought you might gain some insight into what to expect your first year of college. That time is fast approaching! Best wishes!

Love,
Grandma
Jan. 9, 2008

SPARKNOTES is a registered trademark of SparkNotes LLC
SPARKCOLLEGE is a trademark of SparkNotes LLC

Spark Publishing
A Division of Barnes & Noble Publishing
120 Fifth Avenue
New York, NY 10011
www.sparknotes.com

ISBN 13: 978-1-4114-0352-9
ISBN 10: 1-4114-0352-5

Please submit changes or report errors to **www.sparknotes.com/errors**

Printed and bound in Canada.

Library of Congress Cataloging-in-Publication Data available upon request.

CONTENTS

Why 10 Things?

It seems like everyone's writing books that claim to give you the basics, nice and simple—but what you get are pages overstuffed with lots of information you just don't need.

With *10 Things You Gotta Know*, we give you *exactly* what you need—no more, no less. We know you want your knowledge *now*, without wasting time on information that's not important. Learning 10 quick basics is the way to go.

Each 10 *Things* book contains:

- Lots of clear headings for skimming
- Sound bites of text that are easy to digest
- Sidebars that enhance your understanding
- Tons of Top 10 Lists for vital facts at a glance

Sure—maybe you could argue that there are 8 vital things, or 11. This isn't rocket science. But 10 is such a nice, even number—and who doesn't love a great Top 10?

In this book, we focus on the 10 things you absolutely, positively gotta know about surviving your first year of college:

1 **Arriving**

Here we help you figure out what to pack, what not to pack, how to deal with leaving home, what to expect from first-year orientation once you get to college, and how to navigate through your first week in the dorm.

2 **Classes**

Here you'll find all sorts of info about how to sign up for classes and which types of classes you should probably take. You'll also get the low-down on professors, buying books, and how to handle your first semester of academics.

3 **Dorm Life**

Now we're getting to the good stuff: living on your own. Here you'll find out about everything from handling a new roommate to decorating your dorm room. We also cover laundry, food, and how to find a little private time amidst the bustling throng.

4 **Campus Life**

You'll find all sorts of activities and facilities on campus if you know where to look. Knowing how to use them is crucial. This chapter details everything you need to know about the important places to go on campus.

5 **Social Life**

College is nothing if it isn't social. This chapter gives you tips on making friends, joining clubs, going Greek (and crashing their frat parties), the bar scene, and how to stay safe while having fun.

Before we get started, take a look at these 10 questions to see how much you really know about surviving your first year of college. The answers follow.

1 You've just arrived on campus and the butterflies in your stomach are planning a revolt. You've never been so nervous. You:

   A. Tell your folks to turn the car around.

   B. Recognize that this is probably normal and just keep on going. You're sure it will get better.

   C. Feel nauseated and have to get out of the car for some air.

   D. Steady your nerves with the thought of your first college keg party.

2 It's your first day of classes. You expect a small, intimate classroom, but instead you walk into an enormous, noisy lecture hall. You:

   A. Find a seat toward the back. It's the best place to sleep.

   B. Leave. You know you won't get the attention you need in this class.

   C. Take a seat toward the front. Maybe it will feel like a smaller space if you're closer to the professor.

   D. Find the hottest girl/guy and sit next to her/him. You might not learn anything, but at least you'll have a date on Saturday.

3 Drunkenness and debauchery are the themes of your roommate's life. You've never seen this person study, and you're tired of the late-night partying and the homeless-looking strangers in your room every morning. You:

   A. Talk to her about it, but if the behavior doesn't change, you are going to ask to switch rooms.

   B. Pour out all of the alcohol when he isn't home. Then you tell him that the dorm officials did it and that they will be back later to expel him. Watch him squirm.

   C. Try to stick it out. Sophomore year is just nine months away.

   D. Organize an intervention, then hold a rally demanding more campus-wide education about addiction.

4 The library is:

A. The best place to study with no distractions.

B. So quiet. The napping is excellent.

C. A great place to make out.

D. I have no idea.

5 A typical Saturday night for you is:

A. A heated game of Dungeons and Dragons.

B. A big party with friends.

C. Television and some studying, maybe a friend coming over to hang out.

D. You never remember Saturday nights, and you wish you didn't remember Sunday mornings.

6 Binge drinking is:

A. A bad thing to do.

B. A keg or two.

C. More than five drinks in an evening.

D. You don't really know because you black out after four drinks.

7 A credit card company is offering college students a no-fee card and even gives you a free T-shirt for applying. You:

A. Sign up. When the card comes, you go on a shopping spree.

B. Sign up, get the free shirt, and then cut up the card when it arrives.

C. Pass the booth without giving it a second thought—you know you don't want to start accruing debt now.

D. Sign up a few days in a row and give the shirts to your friends for Christmas. You never get the card, since you used a fake name on the application.

8 When the alarm rings in the morning, you:

A. Pull the plug out of the wall and sleep in until 3 P.M.

B. Go get a dozen doughnuts while they're still fresh.

C. What alarm? You've been up all night.

D. Hit snooze once, then get up and do your stretching exercises.

9 When you sit down to study, you:

   A. Don't really "study." You skim.

   B. Immediately think of a million other things you have to do—then you do them.

   C. Remove all distractions and take a break every hour.

   D. Usually fall asleep.

10 Your first year is over! You:

   A. Can't wait to get the heck away from your roommates, especially the one who always smells like cabbage.

   B. Are going to Paris through a summer program to learn French.

   C Buy a new baseball cap. You're going to need it for all the hours you're going to spend mowing lawns for extra cash.

   D. Prepare. Summer classes, here you come.

Answers

1

Answer: B. Your first day of college is going to be a bit nerve-racking, but it will also be one of the most fun and exciting days of your life. If you start with the right attitude, that excitement will last all year. **See Chapter 1.**

2

Answer: C. School can be a lot of fun, but ultimately you are there to learn. Don't make a difficult situation any harder than it has to be. If you find yourself in a giant lecture, take initiative and immerse yourself in the academic environment. **See Chapter 2.**

3

Answer: A. Living with total strangers can be difficult at first. That's why you need to communicate openly with your roommates. If their behavior is making life difficult for you, talk to them about it. Chances are they don't realize how much these things bother you. **See Chapter 3.**

4

Answer: A. Believe it or not, that big building filled with dusty books can actually be a useful resource for college students. Your school realizes that your dorm room isn't the ideal place to get your work done. That's why they've filled the library with hundreds of desks for your studying pleasure. **See Chapter 4.**

5

Answer: B. You thought we were gonna say **C**, didn't you? The key to success in college is balancing fun time with study time. It's OK to take Saturday night off for fun. If you spend all your time studying, you'll miss out on a huge part of the college experience. **See Chapter 5.**

6

Answer: A. As a college student, chances are you're going to be at parties where alcohol will be available. If you decide to drink, make sure you do it responsibly. **See Chapter 6.**

7

Answer: C. Don't give in to the temptation of credit this early in your life! Credit card companies prey on college kids because they know that students are less likely to pay off their charges every month. Be responsible with your money, and you'll have a much easier time maintaining your finances after graduation. **See Chapter 7.**

8

Answer: D. One way to ensure that you stay healthy during your first year is by getting a good night's sleep every night and keeping a regular schedule. Being well rested will do wonders for your grades. **See Chapter 8.**

9

Answer: C. You need to be focused when you study; otherwise, you won't be able to retain anything you learn. Learn how to work for a longer period of time without burning out. **See Chapter 9.**

10

Answer: All of the above. Hey, anything is possible at the end of your first year! Keep your options open for the summer, because there will be a lot of opportunities available to you. Just enjoy whatever you do, because the summer is short, and your sophomore year is just around the corner. **See Chapter 10.**

1
ARRIVING

"Starting college was a real challenge. It was the first time in my life that I didn't have a tight-knit group of friends to lean on. By the third week of school the first-year class had gone through so many new experiences together that we became a close network of people who gave one another strength."

**Tony W.
University of Florida**

10

THINGS

People Are Most
Nervous About

1

Fitting in

2

Liking your roommate

3

Having enough money

4

Finding the dining hall

5

Liking your dorm

6

Being homesick

7

Finding your way around campus

8

Missing your friends

9

Deciding which classes to take

10

Feeling lonely

Steady Your Nerves

OK, you're nervous. That's normal. You'd have to be made of asphalt if you weren't a little edgy. You're away from home and completely unsupervised, probably for the first time in your life. Well, that's the good part. The hard part is being in a foreign place, not knowing anyone, and missing your toothbrush because you forgot which milk crate you put it in.

The good news is that everyone around you is in the same boat. Nobody knows where he or she is going. No one knows where the dining hall is or where the dorm orientation is going to be held. That's OK. Your new school doesn't want you to be freaked out or scared, and it provides countless resources to help you.

"The biggest fear I had was whether or not I'd find anyone like myself at this school. I moved pretty far from my home in the sticks. But the minute I met my roommate I knew I'd be fine— he was exactly like my best friend back home. He even had the same posters!"

David C.
New York University

What to Bring

A major way to relieve the stress of moving into the dorm is to pack appropriately. You will be sorry if you bring things that you won't use, that are too large, or that double up on what your roommate is bringing. Here's a list of the stuff that you'll be very happy to have in your new pad:

10 Things You Gotta Have

1. Computer (don't forget the manuals and software)
2. Power—strip/surge protector, extension cords, and two-to-three prong adaptors
3. Light—desk lamp, floor lamp, and clip lamp
4. Alarm clock (a reliable one!)
5. Laundry supplies—detergent, fabric softener, dryer sheets
6. Hangers
7. Bedding—two sets of sheets and pillowcases, two pillows, one comforter, one fleece blanket (check on sheet size because many dorms have extra-long beds)

8. Toiletries—shampoo, soap, hair brush, toothbrush, toothpaste, etc.
9. Thesaurus and dictionary
10. School supplies—pens, pencils, notebooks, etc.

On top of these items, there are some extra things you should consider bringing if you already own them and you have extra room.

10 Things That Are Nice to Have

1. Television
2. DVD/VCR player
3. Stereo
4. Cell phone and charger
5. Computer printer
6. Photos of family and friends
7. Coffee maker
8. Bicycle
9. A plant
10. Room decorations

What Not to Bring

Every dorm has a list of items they don't allow, and some stuff is just too risky to bring anyway. Here's a list of stuff to leave behind:

10 Things to Leave at Home

1. **Fluffy, Spike, Weasel, Polly, and Kitty.** It's pretty much a guarantee that pets aren't going to be allowed in the dorm. You can ask about it, but don't say we didn't warn you. You may be allowed to have a fishbowl, but check with your dorm first.
2. **Ritzy stuff.** Don't risk having Grandma's ring stolen or losing that fabulous Gucci bag. Yes, you might bring some expensive computer equipment and other gadgets, but those things are replaceable—a family heirloom isn't. If you are bringing expensive computers and gadgets, make sure they are insured and you have the serial numbers written down somewhere safe.

3. **Your whole wardrobe.** If you're moving into the dorm in August, you don't need all of your winter coats and sweaters. You can get these when you go home for Thanksgiving. Remember, your dorm closet looks more like a breadbox than a storage space. Also, college students tend to dress down, so the fashion-show look of some high schools doesn't really fly.

4. **Dry-clean-only clothes.** Don't bring clothes that are too hard to care for. Bring only what you can stuff into a washing machine. If you think you're going to go on job interviews, bring one or two appropriate outfits.

5. **Giant appliances.** Everything in the dorm room should be scaled to size: mini-fridge, plug-in burner (if allowed), and four-cup coffee pots are the norm on campus.

6. **Halogen lamps.** Many colleges consider them a fire hazard and warn students not to bring them.

7. **Your high school yearbook.** It will remind you of home and your friends and might offer you some comfort on those lonely nights. Right? Wrong! It will just take up space, and you won't be looking at it anyway. Your new friends and new activities take up a lot of time, so there will be few spare moments to get misty-eyed and sentimental about high school. Besides, it's fun to look at that stuff at home once you've had some time away from it.

8. **Candles.** Most dorms don't want you setting fires anywhere.

9. **Alcohol.** Most dorms are dry, meaning that alcohol isn't allowed. And, may we add, you're under drinking age anyway.

10. **Drugs.** College kids get busted with drugs all the time too. It's a bad idea to have them and a worse idea to use them.

"I brought so much stuff to school that my parents had to take more than half of it back with them. I had no idea how small the closet was going to be! But it turned out that I didn't even need that stuff anyway."

**Rachel H.
Clemson University**

THINGS

You Can Share with Your Roommate

Packing

If your parents are driving you to school, a trash bag is by far the best disposable suitcase in the world. Yes, you'll look like a refugee pulling up to the dorm with trash bags full of clothes, but if you look around, you'll see that most everyone else has packed in trash bags too. There won't be room in your dorm for a suitcase. If you insist on packing in a suitcase, unpack it immediately (dumping everything on your bed is fine) and give it back to your folks to take home. When you go home for holidays, you'll only need a soft duffle bag, which is easily stored in your closet or under your bed.

If you're driving to campus, you can supplement the garbage-bag suitcases with plastic milk crates. Not only are these great for packing, but you can also see what junk is in which crate. When they're empty they make great shelves, chairs, and footstools. If they take up too much space, they're cheap enough to just toss out.

Shipping Your Stuff

If you're not driving to school, you can pack a lot of stuff in boxes and ship it ahead of time. Make sure to use a company that will track the package. Call your new dorm to make sure that someone will receive the packages and hold them securely for you.

If you're flying, remember that most airlines have a weight limit for suitcases. These days, airport security goes through everything thoroughly, so you may find your nice packing job turned upside down. Your best bet is to send things ahead of time or have your folks send your stuff once you get to school.

Contacting Your Future Roommate(s)

Before you arrive on campus, you should be able to find out the name and phone number of your future roommate. There's a chance you'll be placed in a double, a triple, or a quad, so you may have to make a few phone calls. Expect some phone calls as well, especially if your future roommates get their mail before you do.

Definitely call your roommate(s). It's a great opportunity to introduce yourself and break the ice. It's also a smart idea to discuss who's bringing what; otherwise, you'll find yourself in a small room with three microwaves, two mini-fridges, and four television sets. Excess isn't success.

If you've arranged to have someone you already know as your first-year roommate, then these decisions should be easy. You may even want to go halves on some of the larger-ticket items, like the mini-fridge. Make sure to decide who's going to take (and perhaps keep) the item when you and your roomie part ways for the summer.

Moving In

Keep It to Yourself

There's no way to judge what your first year will be like based on your first day on campus. Try to keep an open mind about your roommates, neighbors, and dorm staff. Write down your first impressions before you say something out loud that you'll end up regretting.

Moving day will be one of the most nerve-racking and exciting days of your life. If you're moving into a dorm, the good news is there will be plenty of people to help you. The dorm should have resident assistants and dorm monitors on hand to guide you to your room, and the dorm should provide you with wheeled bins or hand trucks so you can move your stuff easily.

Once you get to your room and put your stuff down, you'll have to choose a bed and a desk. Which side of the room do you like to sleep on? Do you like to be by a window? Closer to the bathroom? Top bunk or bottom? Ideally, roommates should decide together who's going to get what furniture. If your roomie hasn't arrived yet, just put your stuff to the side and wait till he or she gets there to choose beds. You'll be off to a bad start if you start making executive decisions from the get-go.

Bed Swap

If you get to the room and your new roommate has already claimed a bed and a desk, deal with it if you can. One great way to avoid any conflict is to agree to switch furniture next semester. That way, neither of you will feel too much resentment about having a worse situation. Later on, you might decide there's no need to switch, but it's a nice way to start out the year on even footing.

Goodbye, Folks

Saying goodbye to Mom and Dad might be a tearful scene. That's OK. It's a tearful scene for most people. Just let them be who they are. In a moment, they'll be driving away, and there you'll sit, at the edge of your dorm bed and at the beginning of your adult life.

Make sure to tell your folks that you're going to be OK. You're going to eat regular meals and brush your teeth and study and not do all of the other million things they've warned you about. Oh, and wipe the grin off your face until they've actually driven away.

The First Night

Your dorm will probably have a first-night orientation or social event to welcome you to school. Show up to this—and all—dorm meetings: you'll get to know the people on your floor and make friends quickly.

Unpacking

Unpack as much as you can when you arrive but not at the expense of socializing and meeting other people in the dorm. If you can find your bathroom products and your jammies, you're in good order for the evening.

When you unpack, try to take up only the space allotted to you. You won't score any points with your roommates if you impose on their space. Using stackable crates or stacking plastic bins makes unpacking easy. Get your stuff out of the trash bag and into the bins, and then you can run out for pizza with those cute guys/girls who just moved in across the hall.

Aren't You Sad to See Me Go?

Some parents seem a little too happy to be saying farewell. Don't get bent about it. They're most likely trying to put on a happy face for you. And why shouldn't they be happy? They've raised a good kid who is now a successful adult in college.

 THINGS
To Unpack First

Make sure to put these items on top of everything else you pack.

1
Toothbrush

2
A framed photo from home

3
Toiletries

4
Flip-flops (for the shower)

5
Sheets and bedding

6
Pajamas

7
Snacks

8
Undergarments

9
Next day's clothes

10
Orientation schedule

Finding a Friend

Finding an ally is important. It will help to settle you and is simply more fun than going it alone. Classes haven't started yet, so your social life should be your top priority.

Leaving your dorm room door wide open (with you inside) is a great way to meet people. Students will mill about in the halls, and everyone will mix and mingle in one another's rooms. Many students leave their doors open all the time.

Most dorms also have a common room where you can hang out, talk, read, and have snacks. Check out the common room on your first night. Other first years will be doing the same. The common room is also a great place to bring a board game, which gives you an opportunity to ask someone to play with you. Once a board game gets going, others will want to join in.

The Dining Hall

The dining hall is a great place to meet classmates and make new friends. You're bound to see a recognizable face from the dorm sitting at a table. Don't be shy, and don't sit alone.

If you simply can't muster up the courage to sit with someone you don't know, then sit with a few empty seats around you. Chances are that someone will join you. One quarter of the people around you are first years, and if you're in a first-years' dining hall, they're going through the same nerve-racking experience.

Orientation

During your first week, you'll be attending at least two orientation sessions. One will be a university-wide first-year orientation, parts of which may even include parents. Then, you'll have a housing orientation. If you're in a special program, you'll have an orientation for that too.

Most orientation sessions last several days and include community-building exercises and course selection. Your college will definitely let you know what you need to do and where you need to go. Write everything down, keep whatever the school gives you, and pay attention. These sessions are designed to get you started on the right track. If you're sleeping

ESSENTIAL
Terms

1. **Advisor:** A faculty member (professor) or academic advisor who helps you plan your academic direction.

2. **Academic Probation:** If you don't make good grades, generally falling into "D" territory, the college will put you on academic probation. This generally gives you a semester to improve your grades. If you don't, the college reserves the right to toss you out for a term, a year, or permanently.

3. **Add/Drop:** The "add/drop" period occurs during the first week or two of classes and gives you the chance to withdraw from or add classes with no penalty. After this period, you may still add or drop, but you will be assessed a fee.

4. **Blue Book:** When you take an essay-type test, most professors require you to use a "blue book," which is a small blank booklet that you can buy at the college bookstore. Stock up on these at the beginning of the semester.

5. **Bursar:** The Bursar's Office deals with all the money you pay the college; not to be confused with the Office of Financial Aid, which deals with your loans.

6. **Core Classes:** In the first two years of school, most colleges require you to take specific classes in a variety of academic disciplines.

7. **Electives:** Electives are classes that you choose, which may or may not have anything to do with your major.

8. **Full-time Student:** In most colleges, a full-time student takes at least 12 credit hours per semester.

9. **Resident Assistant/Advisor (RA):** These are juniors, seniors, or graduate students who live in the dorm to enforce rules and help students with campus life.

10. **Registrar:** The registrar's office keeps track of academic records and other student achievements. This is also the office that registers you for classes.

during the session, you'll miss out on important info. This isn't high school: no one's holding your hand anymore.

Housing Orientation

Your dorm will have an important orientation session in the first week, which is often mandatory. You will learn everything about the dorm rules, how to set up your phone service, amenities available to you, safety measures, and other important aspects of living in your particular residence hall.

First-Year Orientation

The university will hold a general first-year orientation, which you should definitely attend and which may be required. You'll find out about important dates, job opportunities, exciting things happening for first years on campus, and anything else you need to know to make the year fun and easy.

You will have to register for first-year orientation so that your school knows how many students are attending.

Parking Permit

If you have a car, you'll need a parking permit. Use your first week to get a parking permit. Some colleges don't allow first years to have the premium permits. You'll find out the scoop when you get to the parking office at your particular university.

Your Student ID

Your student ID is your ticket into campus buildings and your dorm. It might also get you discounts at certain stores, movie theaters, and museums. Use this first week to find the student ID office and get your ID. If you wait too long, the lines will be crazy.

Finding Your Way Around

The first week is a great time to wander around campus and your new town. Your campus will no doubt offer tours, and it's a good idea to find out when they are and take one. Don't worry about getting lost. If you do, you'll find a place that you never would have found if you had a destination. Ask someone to come with you and share the adventure. This is another great way to make friends.

Look in the phone book or online for places that seem interesting. If you're a mall rat, find the local mall, where you're bound to feel at home. Like sports? Find out what your new town offers and then go check it out in person. Whatever you do, don't get caught up in watching TV, playing video games, or instant-messaging people from back home. Start making new memories. It takes effort, but it's worth it. You'll be glad all year that you took your first week to check out your surroundings. Once you feel oriented, you can relax and begin your classes feeling at home.

The Bottom Line

There's a reason why you always hear older people saying, "College was the best time of my life." Or "If only I could relive my college experience . . . " While college truly is a life-changing experience, it is also one of the most fun times of your life. The bottom line on your first week of college is this: relax and have fun. Your new life as a college student is just beginning. This first week (and your first week of classes) is about as stressful as it gets, but if you arrive prepared, you will have a great time.

2 CLASSES

"To those of you who received honors, awards, and distinctions, I say well done. And to the C students, I say you too can be president of the United States."

George W. Bush
43rd President of the United States

Classes: The Reason You're Here

Your first year of college comes with many changes and challenges. Suddenly, *you* have to take care of all these things that were done for you in high school. You've got classes to choose, schedules to arrange, roommates to get along with, and a stomach to feed. Most important, you have to find a way to balance a challenging academic life with an incredibly fun social life. What's a bright-eyed first-year student to do?

Believe it or not, your academic success will greatly enhance your social life. Consider this: a failing student will be put on academic probation or be removed from the university entirely. No more parties. No more 3 A.M. runs for nachos and ice cream at the corner store. Back to your parents' house you go. And won't they be glad to see you! The lawn sure needs mowing after you come home from your twelve-hour shift at McDonald's. *Would you like fries with that?*

Remember, you start college with a clean slate. Your GPA begins with your first class, and you have an opportunity now to prevent your parents from cutting off your pizza cash when those first-semester grades arrive. You'll have a hard time bringing that GPA back up if you party 24/7 your first semester and slack off in class. Try to balance studying with your social life—and by balance, we mean equal parts on *both sides.* Ninety percent partying and 10 percent studying is not a balance; it's a dictatorship, with partying as the despotic king. We're not saying that you'll ruin your life if you let your first-year grades slip. What we are saying is this: you are in college to learn. You and your parents are spending good money on your classes and it's important you get your money's worth.

Choosing Classes

So, you've decided that classes are almost as important as frat parties. Good. Now you have to figure out what classes you're going to take. Many first-year students are clueless about this process. That's where your academic advisor comes in.

Your Academic Advisor

Think of your academic advisor as your lifeline to putting together the best possible schedule for your four-year plan. Some schools require that you meet with an academic advisor in your first year, generally before class registration starts. Even if your school doesn't require a meeting, it would be a mistake not to use this vital resource. Signing up for classes is the most important thing you'll do when you arrive on campus, so be sure to make an appointment with your advisor as soon as possible. You will only need to see the advisor once a term to choose your classes, especially if you're doing well academically. But you may need to see him/her more often if your grades slip or if something comes up that requires you to change your schedule drastically. Your advisor is also the person with whom you're going to discuss your prospective major.

Private Eyes

Your academic advisor is usually not allowed to share any of the information you tell him/her with anyone, not even grades or personal stuff. University officials are often allowed access to your academic information, but your parents and outsiders are not, unless you give consent.

10 Things Your Academic Advisor Does

1. Helps choose your classes
2. Knows what requirements you need to graduate
3. Guides you in choosing a major
4. Serves as the point person for all your academic questions and concerns
5. Helps if you run into academic trouble
6. Helps you develop realistic career goals
7. Monitors your progress, semester by semester
8. Maintains your academic file
9. Informs you of any special services available
10. Refers you to university counseling if you're having a personal problem that's affecting your academics

10 Things Your Academic Advisor Does Not Do

1. Tells you what classes to take
2. Tells you which classes are "good," "bad," "hard," or "easy"
3. Solves problems once they've gone too far
4. Acts as a mediator between you and a professor
5. Helps you solve nonacademic issues, such as housing
6. Acts as a personal counselor
7. Serves as a mediator between you and classmates or dormmates
8. Helps you with your schoolwork
9. Takes responsibility for your academic achievement (or lack thereof)
10. Enforces campus rules and regulations

Classes You Gotta Take

Your university has core requirements that you'll need to take (and pass) before you can graduate; most of the time you won't even be able to move on to higher-level classes until you pass these core classes. English is a big core requirement, and you'll probably have to take more than one section of it. You may also have to take a foreign language, science, math, physical education, or history. It's a good idea to get many of these requirements out of the way as soon as possible, but don't get swamped with so much work that you let your grades slip. Remember, you're adjusting to college life and all of its challenges.

The placement exams you took in high school, such as the SAT Subject Tests and APs, may fulfill some of your core requirements—if you scored high in certain exams, you may not have to take some subjects. Your school may also offer tests that get you out of some requirements, like a foreign language. Ask your academic advisor about what you can do to skip some of the core classes and move on to your electives.

Electives

Electives are classes that you're not required to take but that either fulfill the requirements for your prospective major or simply earn you the credits you need to graduate. If you're allowed a couple of electives in your first year, choose something that interests you instead of trying to rack up credits for your major. Chances are you won't even know yet what your major is.

One of the great things about your first year is that it is a time for academic discovery. Don't be afraid to take electives that sound strange or that aren't related to your most obvious interests. The wider you cast your net, the more options you'll have when it comes time to pick a major. Who knows? That course on ancient Mesopotamian architecture could lead to a rewarding major in archaeology.

The Course Catalog

Every semester your school will print a course catalog (sometimes called a *course bulletin*) that lists classes being offered that term and gives a little synopsis of each class. The synopsis should tell you what to expect in the class, so be sure to read the catalog carefully before registering.

In general, each class has a code made up of letters and numbers. The letters correspond to the department that offers the class. For example, *ENG* stands for the English department, *ACC* for accounting, and *CHM* for chemistry. The numbers will often tell you what level the class is: ENG101 is beginning English. In addition, the catalog will list the days and times the class is scheduled and how many credits you'll receive for taking the class. Each college has its own system of numbering and lettering classes. Once you get the hang of reading the catalog, it'll be easy to find the classes you want and need.

Writing Courses

Learning how to write effectively is a key to college success. Most schools offer writing-intensive classes that are only open to first-year students. If your writing isn't up to speed, the professors who teach these courses will help you perfect the art of writing a college paper.

Here's what a catalog listing might look like:

HIST101

U.S. History to 1865: This course will examine the central themes, events, and ideas that shaped U.S. history, from the colonial period to the end of the Civil War. Students must sign up for lecture and one section. No prerequisites.

Enrollment: 50

Lecture: MWF 9:00–10:00 A.M.	4 Credits
Section 01: M 10:00–11:00 A.M.	1 Credit
Section 02: T 10:00–11:00 A.M.	1 Credit
Section 03: W 10:00–11:00 A.M.	1 Credit

The Chatty Professor

Your professors went to graduate school to study the topic they're teaching, and they love to talk about their work. Chatting with your professors gives them the opportunity to get to know you. Can this sway grades? You bet.

The 3-1 Rule

You will need about three hours of study time per week for each credit you take. If you're taking 24 credits, you'll have to schedule 72 study hours; make sure you have enough time in your week to allow for that. College is much more challenging than high school, where you were able to take seven classes a day, write for the school newspaper, and play a varsity sport. College professors expect more from you than your high school teachers did. If you're taking two challenging classes, make sure you balance your schedule with two classes that have lighter workloads.

Your Professors

You're probably picturing professors as intimidating, frumpy old men who smell like mothballs. There's a slight chance you'll end up with one or two profs who fit this profile, but most of the people who teach your classes will be engaging, passionate academics who really want you to succeed. Most college professors will treat you like a colleague as long as you offer them the same respect. You may not have wanted to get to know your high school teachers, but you'll want to get to know some of your college profs. Go to their office hours just to say hello and introduce yourself.

By the time you register, you will probably have heard a lot of horror stories about some of the professors who teach first-year courses. Don't let these stories sway you too much. Consider the source: a professor that "grades hard" might just have graded your brother's slacker friend appropriately. Take the classes that you agree upon with your advisor and that fit well into your schedule.

Class Size

If you go to a large school, some of your core classes will be huge lectures with hundreds of students. In addition to the professor, a few teaching assistants will be on hand. Try to sit at the very front, nearest to the professor. If you don't, you may find yourself distracted and unable to follow what's being taught.

A smaller, more intimate class is called a *seminar*. Both core classes and electives can be taught seminar-style. Smaller liberal arts colleges hold most of their classes as seminars. Large colleges have fewer seminars for their first years and sophomores. If you attend a large school, you'll probably have more seminars once you choose your major.

If you plan well, you'll end up with a mix of seminars and large lectures your first year. If you feel comfortable with a particular topic and did well in it in high school, then a large lecture might suit you. If you're wary about a particular topic and feel you may need more attention in the class, try to find a seminar.

Registration Day

Now that you've considered all the possibilities, it's time to make things official by actually registering for your classes. You'll have to fill out some forms before you register, which you can get from your academic advisor or from the registrar's office. Some schools make you come to campus and stand in line to register, either with a person or via computer. Other colleges allow you to register over the phone or at computer stations on

10

Preregistration Questions

1 **Is the class a requirement or an elective?** In your first year, you'll want to get at least four requirements out of the way; some schools insist on even more.

2 **Is the class in a good time slot?** If you're a night person, don't choose an 8 A.M. class. Can you get to the class on time considering your work schedule, other classes, and distance to travel?

3 **Have you heard good things about the professor?** Bad things? Substantiate rumors before you eliminate a class, and don't sign up for a class just because you heard that the prof always gives good grades.

4 **Do you have a lot of tough classes in your schedule already?** Adding another difficult class isn't going to make your life any easier. Consider balancing your schedule between challenging and easier classes.

5 **Are you picking a class just because your friends are taking it?** Choosing a class for this reason is a bad idea. Look for classes that suit your own interests.

6 **Is the class already full?** If you get shut out of an important class, attend the first class meeting and ask the professor if it would be possible to override the system to let you in.

7 **Do you know enough about the class?** Before you sign up for a class, you should visit the prof during office hours. You'll get a vibe from the him/her that may help you decide whether to take the class. Ask to see the syllabus if possible, and ask about texts, workload, and class content. Remember, be polite.

8 **Do any of your classes count toward your major?** If you're already thinking about a particular major, find out what the prerequisites and requirements are and start taking some of those classes.

9 **Is your schedule balanced?** You don't want to take all math classes or all English classes in your first term. A couple of requirements and some interesting electives would make a well-rounded schedule.

10 **Are all your classes reading/writing intensive?** Some classes require a lot of reading, some require a lot of writing, and some require a lot of both. Try to find out what each class entails and don't swamp yourself with too many classes that require a similar workload.

campus. Registration is easy: people will be around to help you, and you will be given explicit instructions to follow.

In a perfect world, you'll get into your top four classes, but there are no such guarantees in the real world. You should always choose a few alternate classes in case your first choices are full by the time you register. One important rule is: *register early*. No matter what, you'll probably get at least two of the classes you really want, but if you register early, you may get them all.

The First Day of Classes

Now that you're equipped with the perfect schedule, it's time to get up and go to class. When the first day arrives, give yourself enough time to perform all your morning rituals. You're going to be excited and a little nervous about your first class, which is totally natural. Just stay calm and you'll make it through the day. And ask for help when you need it: every student on campus has experienced what you're going through, and they will all be able to guide you through your first day.

Finding Your Classes

The first thing you have to do is *find* your first class. Most colleges are pretty big; even small schools have several classroom buildings, just enough to make things confusing. Don't be afraid to ask someone where your class is: either they'll tell you where to go, or they'll be a lost first year just like you, in which case you might even make a new friend. You should have received a campus map during orientation week. If not, you can stop by the student center and pick one up. Most schools also have campus maps online.

Be on Time

Many professors will understand when a first year is late on day one; after all, you don't know where you're going. Unfortunately, a few instructors can be pretty brutal about tardiness, so if you're smart, you'll have practiced your schedule beforehand.

Keeping Track of Time

The first thing you may notice is that there are no bells before or after a class. There's nothing to signal when classes begin or end, except maybe for the commotion on campus when classes let out—but you can't even count on that. The only thing you can count on is the watch on your wrist (or that little clock on your cell phone), so make sure that it's always set to the right time.

Keep a copy of your schedule with you, including the dates, times, and locations of your classes. You may want to keep a few copies of your schedule handy: one in your dorm room, one in your backpack, and one in your purse or gym bag.

Class Structure

If your first class is in a big lecture hall, your professor will probably drone into a microphone while you furiously take notes. Don't start daydreaming or you may miss something important. If the class is in a small seminar room, the professor might start class by lecturing for a while before starting a discussion.

Some classes are a blend of lecture and seminar. You may have a large lecture once a week with a professor, then a couple of seminar classes with a graduate student later in the week that elaborate on the lecture.

The Course Syllabus

Your instructor will pass out a syllabus on the first day of class. This document contains all of the important information you need to know about the class, including these 10 things:

1. Professor's name
2. Office hours
3. Phone number and email address
4. Classroom

> "You get used to classes really quickly. There's no reason to panic. After the first couple of weeks, you know where you're going, what you're doing, and you're set."
>
> **Leslie F.**
> **SUNY Purchase**

5. Description of the class
6. Class requirements
7. Grade requirements
8. Absence and tardiness policy
9. Reading and test schedule
10. Important due dates

This is a *very* important document to keep. The course syllabus is the contract between you and your professor. Sometimes, professors will have students sign a copy of the syllabus and give it back. They do this so you can't complain later that you didn't know when the tests were or what the attendance policy was. Make a copy of each of your syllabi. Keep one copy with you and one in your room.

In-Class Behavior

To make a good impression on your professors and classmates, follow these 10 rules:

1. Always be quiet. No one wants to listen to you yap during class.
2. Take notes. The professor is not talking just to hear his/her own voice. What your prof says in class will definitely be important when finals come around.
3. Save social interactions for outside of class. Most professors will not tolerate disruptive behavior.
4. Don't pass notes, throw things, or behave like a fool in any way, shape, or form. You can be a fool on your own time and on your own dime. Other people are there to learn.
5. Turn off your cell phone or put it on vibrate. And if it does vibrate, don't answer it!
6. Keep your shoes on. It's rude and smelly to remove them.

Bathroom Breaks

Unlike high school, you don't have to ask permission to go to the bathroom. Just get up quietly and go, then come back as quietly as you can. It's not a big deal, as long as you don't disrupt the class.

7. Don't chew gum, or at least don't chew it loudly. In a large lecture hall, any repetitive sound—especially one as annoying as someone smacking gum—will stick out.

8. No public displays of affection. Don't make out or play footsy with that special someone; you'll be out of class soon enough.

9. Keep smartass (and dumbass) remarks to yourself. Unless your professor creates an atmosphere where a little kidding around is tolerated, you should keep your "witty" remarks to yourself.

10. Don't fall asleep. There is nothing more disrespectful than falling asleep while your professor is teaching. Profs spend hours preparing lectures and classroom discussion; show a little courtesy and stay awake.

To Buy or Not to Buy

Avoid buying optional books until after the first day of classes, when you'll have a better sense of what you really need. Textbooks are very expensive, so you want to avoid the additional expense if you can.

Buying Your Books

You can buy your books from the campus bookstore before classes begin. You'll find your class listed on a card attached to a shelf in the bookstore. Usually, the shelves are stacked alphabetically by department, so all the accounting books will be on one shelf, all the history books on another . . . all the way down to zoology. Some books will be "optional," meaning that your professor isn't requiring you to buy them. New books should cost you about $400 a semester.

Buy your books as soon as you know which classes you're taking. The bookstore becomes a zoo once classes start, and you'll be ticked off waiting in a two-hour line while holding fifty pounds of books. If you buy the wrong book or drop a class, you can usually make a return, so keep your receipt. Most campus bookstores (and those nearby that serve campuses) have return deadlines, so be sure to ask about the return policy.

Used Books

Fortunately, most campus bookstores do sell used books, which can cut your costs by about 30 percent. You can generally find used books online at **www.bncollege.com**. The cool thing about used books is that someone has generally highlighted the important stuff for you and made notes in the margins. Of course, some moron may have had the book before you and highlighted all of the wrong stuff, so don't rely entirely on someone else's study skills—or lack thereof. You can usually sell your books back at the end of the term, unless they're too defaced or wrecked to be used again.

Grades and Your GPA

It's easy to let grades slip that first semester. There are so many events going on and so much partying to do. And let's not forget how difficult some of your classes will be. Do your best to keep up your grades. Bad grades in your first year will bring down your total grade point average. You'll probably be a better student in your junior and senior years, when you're working on your major, and you'll be pretty mad at yourself if the only thing killing your GPA is a bad grade or two from your first year.

Dropping Classes

Unlike high school, you can drop college classes and either pick up new ones or take fewer than you intended. Each semester has a "no penalty" drop/add date close to the beginning of the semester. Be sure to drop and add classes before that date if you want a full refund or if you want to swap classes. There will be other drop dates, but those come with financial penalties. As the semester goes on, you'll be charged more for dropping a class. For example, three weeks into the semester, the school may

Calling in Sick

If you're sick, don't hesitate to skip class and stay in bed. If you try to drag your sick butt to class, you're only going to succeed in spreading around your germs and making yourself feel worse. Your professors and classmates will be grateful not to have a sniffling germ-factory disrupting class.

10

TIPS

For the First Day of Classes

1. Practice your schedule, going from class to class a few days before the big day. That way you'll know how long it takes to move to and from classes, and you'll already know where your classes are.

2. Get to know someone in each of your classes. You won't necessarily make friends the first day, but it's important to lay the groundwork. Knowing someone in each of your classes is invaluable: you can exchange notes, find out what happened when you were absent, and study together.

3. Organize your class materials. You should have a folder or organizer for each class.

4. Write down everything your professors say (well, maybe not everything, but at least as much as you can). The first day is chock-full of information you'll need all semester.

5. Make a photocopy of your class syllabi. Carry one copy with you and tack the other one to your bulletin board. You'll be glad later that you did this.

6. Put all due dates into your organizer/calendar, and highlight all of the course requirements on your syllabus.

7. If there's something the professor asks the class to do for the next class, do it that night so you don't begin the term by falling behind. Yes, the dorm party is important too, but go only after you've made a dent in your homework.

8. Take a snack with you to class, as well as a bottle of water (or some other non-carbonated beverage, so it doesn't make noise when you open it). You might not have time for lunch, and hunger isn't good for concentration (or nerves).

9. Avoid the bookstore if you can. The lines will be insanely·long on the first day of classes. Instead, try to get up early the next day and wait at the bookstore when it opens. Also, check to see if you can get any of your books at another store: many used bookstores open near campus for just this purpose.

10. Don't get too overwhelmed. Just breathe and try not to get frustrated. Take a moment to look at other people on campus; the other first years are in the same position you're in, and everyone else was in your shoes on their first day too.

only refund 75 percent of the class fee; four weeks into the semester, you might only get 50 percent back. Some colleges require the professor to sign a drop form.

One way to avoid killing your GPA is to drop a class you're doing terribly in, even if that means losing the money you spent on it. There's a deadline to do this as well, and once the drop deadline has passed, you're stuck with the grade. Your transcript will show every add/drop, and you don't want a future graduate school or employer to see too much of that. Some colleges have a "repeat" option that you can use a certain number of times in case you fail a class. You can retake the class and replace the failing grade with a passing one. The failing class will still show up on your transcript, but the F will not factor into your overall GPA.

Incompletes

If you're doing poorly in a class or have to quit a class because of some other factor out of your control (like illness or work), you can take an incomplete. You won't get a grade for the class, nor will your transcript reflect a dropped class. Your transcript will show a placeholder (like an *I*) instead of a grade. You have to make arrangements with a professor to make up the work or tests in the class, usually by the next term.

Whether you can take an incomplete is totally up to your professor. Generally, explaining that you've been ill or have taken on too much that term is good enough for most profs. Check out your school's policy at the registrar's office. If you stop going to class, your professor will not withdraw you automatically. Instead, you will get a failing grade. In some cases, a professor is allowed to give a "no grade" placeholder if you don't show up for something important, like the final exam. This placeholder will turn into an F if you don't contact the professor and remedy the situation.

Class Courtesy

If you have to leave early from a smaller class, tell the professor ahead of time. You don't have to explain why you're leaving, so don't lie about a doctor's appointment. Certainly don't mention that you're leaving class to work on your tan.

REASONS
To Take an Incomplete

1

You get sick at the end of the semester.

2

You have a family emergency.

3

You have too many work obligations.

4

You're in a theater production during finals week.

5

You're playing in the "big game" the same day as the final.

6

You haven't finished your coursework.

7

You can't drop the class because you need it for your major.

8

You have two finals scheduled for the same day.

9

You need the semester break to study up for the final.

10

You have a research project that needs extra attention.

DORM LIFE

"Dorm living? I have two words that will save your life: storage cubes."

**Rachel K.
Tulane University**

REASONS
To Live On Campus

1

Your college may require it.

2

You'll meet more people.

3

The dining hall is right downstairs.

4

You won't need a car, since everything is within walking distance.

5

Free pizza and ice cream nights.

6

Study groups are easier to find.

7

The laundry room is down the hall.

8

You'll live near your friends.

9

The gym is nearby.

10

You'll get to participate in fun dorm activities and campuswide dorm competitions.

Life On Campus

According to several really important-sounding studies, first-year students living on campus perform better academically than those who live off campus. Perhaps it's because students living in dorms are closer to the things they need, like the library and the computer labs. Or maybe it's because the meal plan that comes with most dorms takes the pressure off having to forage for food, giving students more time to study. And think of all the potential study partners floating around the hallways or energetically highlighting their textbooks in the study lounge. No wonder dorm life for first years is such a good idea.

On Campus or Off Campus?

Should you live in a dorm your first year? In a word: yes. Socially, you can't beat dorm living. You'll make friends easily, commiserate about school with your dormmates, study with groups of friends, always have someone to eat with, and stay up late socializing almost every night. You will share your college experience with other people who are going through the same ups and downs, and that makes everything easier. There is great strength in numbers.

Studying can be difficult in a dorm, because socializing often takes priority over grades. But you can easily balance this by heading to the library or to a quiet study hall.

All of these advantages don't erase the fact that dorm life can be challenging. You're living in close proximity to a lot of other people, and that's a recipe for conflict. But conflict is part of life, and learning how to deal with it successfully is essential to becoming an adult.

The Dorm

Not all dorm rooms resemble dark, damp prison cells. Some are downright luxurious, looking more like plush apartment suites than campus housing. Some colleges have a lot of money to spend on housing, and their dorms tend to be more livable. Other campuses might not have the cash flow to put into the dorms, so you might find yourself living between four thickly painted cinderblock walls, with nothing but a lumpy mattress to cry on when the toilets clog up—again. But it's usually not that bleak. Sometimes

10

Dorm Choices

1. **Single gender.** All-girl and all-guy dorms have very different cultures. Girls stay up all night talking. Guys stay up all night playing video games and wishing the dorm were coed. There tend to be fewer all-male dorms than all-female (so relax, guys). The disadvantage of a single-gender dorm is the fun factor. It's simply more exciting to be in a coed dorm. Also, coed dorms eliminate the mystique of the opposite sex. When you're living with both guys and girls, everyone becomes just another person in the hallway.

2. **Coed by room.** Many dorms are coed by room: girls and guys sharing walls but not rooms. Exciting at first, yes. However, this excitement can quickly turn sour when romantic relationships in the dorm go bad.

3. **Single-gender floors.** Some dorms are coed but split the girls and guys up by floor. Depending on dorm rules, you may or may not be able to mix after certain hours.

4. **Sexual orientation.** Many universities have floors devoted to gay, lesbian, and transgender students, as well as anyone else who identifies with these orientations.

5. **All first year.** Some dorms are set aside for first-year students only. The benefit: no juniors or seniors ticked off by all the noise and chaos.

6. **Quiet floors.** Often, dorms will set aside quiet floors where it's easier to study. The fear is that the residents on these floors are uptight and won't party, but that's not always the case. They just don't want the party in their faces. However, quiet is relative to the listener, and many people will find these floors noisy, especially if the rules aren't well enforced.

7. **Substance-free.** These dorms or floors are for people who don't drink or take drugs; additionally, drunk or wasted kids aren't allowed inside.

8. **Special focus.** Some campuses offer special dorm floors, such as those for students with an interest in majoring in music or languages or are dedicated to earning academic honors.

9. **Special housing for disabled students.** These dorms or floors are equipped to accommodate students with disabilities.

10. **International dorms.** Some colleges have dorms specifically for students from other countries. Domestic students are allowed to live in these dorms too, but priority is given to those students coming from abroad.

when the dorms in big urban colleges fill up, schools house their students in luxury hotels. Room service, maids . . . imagine the possibilities.

You don't have a lot of choice when it comes to where you're going to live. You will probably be asked to fill out a form indicating your housing choices. You can list your *ideal* dorms on campus (if you've visited or done some research), but there's no guarantee that you'll end up there. Some campuses have first-year–only dorms, in which case you'll have a better idea of where you'll end up.

Types of Rooms

Most first years will have at least one roommate. It is possible to get a *single*, where you live alone, but the chances are slim. The *double* is the most common arrangement, where two people share a room. Some dorms are made of *suites*, which are basically two or more rooms in an apartment, with two students in each room. Suites often include a shared bathroom, a common area, and sometimes a kitchen area. As enrollment rises at many schools, doubles are often turned into *triples* or *quads*, so don't be surprised if you end up with more than one roommate.

Communal Bathrooms

Communal bathrooms are, well, an experience. If you have a lot of siblings, you're not particularly shy, or you don't mind sharing your space, the communal bathroom experience shouldn't bother you too much. If you're not used to having your privacy invaded, you'll have a lot more adjusting to do.

Many halls will only have one bathroom for guys and one for girls, meaning that twenty-eight girls may need to shower all at the same time. But this rarely happens. Everyone's schedule is different, so you shouldn't have to wait too long to soap up. Some bathrooms are coed, which means you may be competing with everyone on the floor for mirror space. And heaven help you if you have a crush on someone down the hall. He or she will see you at your less-than-finest moments. Bed head can be sexy, but not when it has twigs and beer in it. But perhaps the object of your affection will catch you on a night when you're looking pretty hot. Do people ever get busy in the coed bathrooms? Um, *yeah*, but not as often as you'd think.

Keeping It Clean

Dorms with suite-style housing generally have bathrooms in each room, so you'll only have to share with your roommates. Come up with a cleaning schedule, and if all of you follow it, the bathroom should remain fungus-free.

All you really need to keep a bathroom clean is a jug of bleach, a can of abrasive cleanser (or baking soda), a sponge, a bucket, and some rubber gloves, the kind used for washing dishes. A 10 percent bleach/90 percent water solution kills most germs. The abrasive cleanser will get the soap scum off the bathtub or shower. Use the gloves when you clean, because you won't like what it does to your skin.

Noise

Unless you're on a designated quiet floor, the dorm is probably going to be very noisy. There's always a lot going on: blaring music, noisy games, television, people laughing and talking, and general mayhem in the halls. Many people leave their doors open (which is not a great idea—we'll explain why later), so everyone mingles in and out of the rooms. Although most dorms insist on quiet after ten or eleven at night, your roommate might get on the phone with her best friend back home and start an hour-long conversation about chronic acne. Or your roommate might be engaged in a hook-up session with his "girlfriend" of the week.

If you're trying to sleep or study, consider a portable white-noise machine. There are small units on the market that you can put in your pocket or under your pillow and listen to with earphones. It'll drown out noise with the sound of rain, a babbling brook, or any number of other nature sounds. Of course, some people find these noises annoying too. Can you study or sleep to music? Try that. Soft earplugs aren't noise-proof, but they do block a considerable amount of background noise. If you snore or are the noisy one in your room, offer to buy your roommate some earplugs and do your best to be considerate.

Dos and Don'ts

Dorms have a lot of rules, especially dorms inhabited by first years. Here are some of the rules you may face in your campus housing. These vary, obviously, by school and individual dorm.

10 Common Dorm Rules

1. **No alcohol.** Some dorms allow students who are over 21 to have alcohol in their rooms. As a first year, you are probably not over 21.

2. **No fire hazards.** These include candles, incense, cigarettes, portable heating units, and sometimes halogen lamps and irons. Some dorms still have smoking rooms, but this is becoming less common.

3. **No unruly conduct.** In other words, no fighting, destroying dorm property, setting off fire alarms . . . you get the idea.

4. **No weapons.** Even paintball guns, darts, and archery equipment may be banned.

5. **No members of the opposite sex.** In dorms that house only one gender or on dorm floors with only one gender, there may be rules about having the opposite sex in your room past a certain hour, and some dorms don't allow the opposite sex there at all.

6. **No holes in the walls and ceilings.** Each dorm will interpret this rule differently. Some will allow a certain number of holes, and some will allow as many thumbtacks as you want to use, but no nails.

7. **No pets.** Leave them at home with your parents.

8. **No appliances.** Some dorms have rules about what kinds of kitchen items you can bring. Some only allow low-wattage microwaves and coffeemakers, and others don't allow anything, not even a little fridge. Check with your dorm before you bring any appliances.

9. **No loud music or voices at night.** Quiet hours generally start at 10 or 11 P.M. No loud music or voices after this time.

10. **No new roommates.** No one else can live in your dorm room but you and your roommate(s).

Older First Years

If you're over 21, married, or a single parent, most colleges will exempt you from living in the dorms. But some colleges do have family housing that may be able to accommodate students in these situations.

WAYS
To Block Out Noise

1. Soft foam earplugs from the drugstore are great for blocking background noise and soft snoring.

2. Musician's earplugs can be custom fit for your ears, but they can be expensive.

3. A small white-noise machine or white-noise CD with ear buds blocks just about anything you don't want to hear.

4. Wear headphones or ear buds and play music of your choice.

5. Nature CDs (thunderstorms, rain, rainforest) block out a lot of unwanted noise.

6. Ear protectors worn by hunters and at the shooting range block background noise and muffle louder noises.

7. Stack your pillows. Insert your head between layers.

8. Hardware stores generally carry ear protection for people using leaf-blowers.

9. In a pinch, turn on the radio and find some good static: this is the poor man's white-noise machine.

10. Wearing winter earmuffs will block some background noise.

Security

First years often have an open-door policy in the dorm, which is a good way to encourage your local kleptomaniac to steal your stuff. Keep your door locked. If you have a desktop computer, laptop, or other electronic equipment, keep it tethered to something solid using a security cable, which you can purchase at any computer store. This doesn't absolutely prevent someone from stealing your stuff, but it's a deterrent.

A locked footlocker or small trunk is another great way to deter theft. Stick a lamp and a couple of books on top, and you've got a nightstand that no one will suspect contains your $1,600 laptop. This is better than a safe when it comes to dorm room security. If you bring a safe, you can pretty much guarantee that a group of your dormmates are going to walk off with it as a prank. A safe is pretty easy to carry away; a locked trunk isn't. You may even be able to get a trunk with your school colors and insignia on it.

Personal Safety

Worse things can happen than someone stealing a laptop or phone cards if there's a security lapse in the dorm. Sexual assaults, battery, and other assorted felonies can take place if students keep their doors and windows unlocked or if they let strangers into the dorm when entering and exiting.

Campus security can be pretty good, but dorm security is often left up to the resident assistants (known as RAs), who aren't the best watchdogs. If your roommate asks you to leave the door open because he/she lost a key, suggest that you both contact your RA and get a new lock and keys immediately. It's not your problem when your roommate loses his/her keys. It *is* your problem when a violent stranger walks into your room at night. Also, be careful and alert when going to the communal bathroom at night.

Hiding in Plain Sight

If you want to hide something small, like jewelry or money, try a diversion safe, which is a container that looks like a common household cleaner, food item, or potted plant. Don't let your roommate know about your diversion safe, but make sure that he/she doesn't tamper with the container thinking that it's mayonnaise or tile cleaner.

Fire Safety

Never, ever ignore a fire alarm in your dorm. Fires are very common in dorms, often caused by smoking, illegal candle use, cooking, or overloading electrical outlets. Every year students die in dorm fires because they disable the fire alarm in their rooms. Read your dorm's fire plan and get to know all of the exits. Ignoring a fire drill might be tempting, especially in the middle of the night in the winter, but you never know when it might be the real thing.

Greek Housing

If you're counting on joining a fraternity or sorority, you're in for a distinctly different housing experience. Most Greek houses are large, some accommodating more than a hundred members. Often, there are large sleeping rooms, generally one that's kept at a cooler temperature and one that's kept warmer. All your personal items are stored in a separate area. Alternatively, members are housed together in rooms, usually more than two to a room. Sometimes, frats and sororities take a floor or two in a regular dorm.

What you give up in privacy with Greek housing, you make up for in amenities. Each house has its own cook, with homemade meals prepared each day. Laundry facilities may be in the house, as well as a gym and a computer area. But you also give up living the coed lifestyle, so be prepared to spend a lot of time with the guys/girls in your new Greek family. You will also be expected to participate in many house activities, which would otherwise be your free time if you lived in the dorm, and sleep can be hard to come by. But the camaraderie of your brothers/sisters can't be had in the dorm.

Your Room

Your room should be a reflection of your personality, but it should also be comfortable for your roommate. Before you begin rearranging furniture and putting up posters, have a meeting with your roommate about how you're going to decorate. Make it fun by scheduling a decorating night where you gather all of your decorating materials and try to make everything come together to create a décor. Or, if you're not that inspired, you can just agree to hang on your side of the room, but make sure you consult your roommate first, just to keep the peace.

Lighting

Most dorm lighting is fluorescent and insufficient. Bring low-wattage lamps with you, especially one for your desk. Clip-on lamps are nice, because they are versatile and you can aim them anywhere. Use full-spectrum light bulbs if you're in a town where the winters are dreary. If you're in Arizona or South Florida . . . well, we don't feel sorry for you. Go to the pool and get some sun.

Decorating

Dorm decoration is as individual as the people living in the rooms. Most roommates will decide on a décor plan together, which can be a fun bonding experience. But others will just decorate their own space however they like. One thing's for sure: dorm décor is by far some of the most inventive and innovative interior decoration you'll ever see. You will never have a room decorated like this again, so have some fun with it.

Most dorms do not allow you to paint, put nails or screws in the walls, make holes in the walls, or attach anything anywhere. Keeping these restrictive rules in mind, here are some tips for easy and inexpensive dorm room décor, including a few things to avoid:

10 Decorating Tips

1. Privacy is always a problem in small dorm rooms. Tacking up attractive fabric to bunk beds is a great way to make a little haven for yourself.
2. Use mirrors to make the room look larger.
3. Guys: it's tempting to hang up a ton of girly posters, but any real girls who come to your room might peg you for a pervert.

Toothpaste Touch-ups

If you do make holes in your walls, make sure to spackle them when you leave. Do not use toothpaste to fill in the holes. RAs are savvy to this tactic; they probably did it themselves at the end of their first year. Remember, you will get charged for whatever damage you do to the room.

TIPS

To Make Your Dorm Room More Comfortable

1

If your bed isn't comfy, buy a foam or feather topper for it.

2

If your desk is too small, consider buying a two-drawer filing cabinet.

3

Use fabric and tacks to create privacy curtains.

4

Use full-spectrum light bulbs.

5

Buy dark curtains or a dark shower curtain to block the sun in the morning.

6

Buy a small fan to circulate air.

7

Put up some photos of home.

8

Get a fish tank and some fish (if allowed).

9

Stock up on snacks.

10

Get along with your roommate!

4. Since you won't be able to paint (not without being penalized, anyway), try hanging up fabric using liquid starch (which you can get at craft stores). Soak 18-inch fabric squares in the starch and paste them to the walls using a sponge. When you're moving out, simply remove the fabric with a bucket of water and a sponge.

5. Glow-in-the-dark stars transform a room into the night sky in just a few minutes, but realize that those stars are hard to get off the ceiling and walls. Instead, use the larger stars and planets that can be applied with putty. Or buy clear vellum paper and cut it into circles, then string the circles onto fishing wire; apply the stars to the vellum, then hang the fishing wire all over the room using small thumbtacks.

6. Christmas lights are a dorm favorite. The multicolored ones might be a bit much for your dorm room, so consider the plain white or blue lights.

7. A lot of roommates decide on a theme. First-year guys tend to create alcohol-themed rooms, putting up bottles, neon signs, liquor posters, and so on. Girls often create color-themed rooms, focusing on shades of one color or variations on one pattern.

8. Yellow caution tape (like the stuff the police use) is popular with first years. You'll never use this stuff to decorate with again, so you might as well get it out of your system now.

9. Use contact paper to cover dull or damaged furniture surfaces.

10. Get a nice piece of fabric or a sheet to cover up that ugly, standard-issue, stained dorm-room couch.

Your own space is limited in your room, so make it count. Buy a nice, plush comforter for your bed and some throw pillows (yes, even for the guys). Most dorm residents go with the "lots of stuff on the walls" approach, so make your own space reflect your personality by putting up postcards and objects cut from magazines. Use removable putty to apply everything to your walls.

The Element of Surprise

Should you live with someone you already know? Maybe a friend from home? Most people would say no because you risk ruining the friendship. You also miss out on meeting someone new. The elements of surprise and anticipation are part of the first-year experience.

Surviving Your Roommate

Many roommates become the best of friends, while many others spend the year resenting and hating one another. Some share everything; others opt for the "tape across the room" style of living, where the room is halved and neither roommate can invade the other's space. Unless you request to live with a friend, you don't know who you're going to get. But your school does its best to pair you up with someone compatible based on the survey you fill out when you apply to live in the dorms. You will probably be asked:

1. If you smoke
2. What time you go to bed
3. What time you get up in the morning
4. If you're messy or clean
5. If you like to play music while studying
6. What kind of music you like
7. What your expectations are for school
8. How you like to de-stress
9. What your interests are
10. If you will have a lot of guests

Your roommate will be the same gender as you unless your college is progressive and you agree to a coed suite. You won't automatically get matched with someone of the opposite sex in your first year, and you will always know ahead of time what you're signing on for when you apply to live in the dorms each subsequent year.

Do Unto Others . . .

The first rule of being a good roommate is to be considerate. Yeah, we know, it's not always easy. But the best way to get what you want is to allow the other person to have what he/she wants too. It's called compromise. If you don't do anything to step on your roommate's toes, you have a lot of leverage if he/she steps on yours. Instead of living in a constant tug-of-war, be nice and accommodating from the start. If you start out on a bad note, it can last all year.

House Rules

Once you've settled in, make an appointment with your roommate as soon as possible to order pizza and talk about how you're going to live together. Here are some important points to consider:

10 Things to Discuss with Your Roommates

1. **The phone.** How are you going to handle messages? What's the limit for conversations if someone is waiting for the phone? What's the cut-off time for incoming calls?

2. **Noise.** What time do you turn off music? How late can you party with your friends in the room?

3. **Schedule.** When is lights out? When do you open the curtains in the morning? When do you like to study?

4. **Open door.** Is your door going to be locked or open most of the time? (We recommend locking it.)

5. **Neatness.** How clean do you like your space? Will you set up a cleaning schedule and agree to pick up after yourselves?

6. **Borrowing.** Are some things off-limits? Do you need to ask before borrowing something, or can you just use it? What if something gets broken or lost?

7. **Food.** If there will be food in the room, are you going to split it?

8. **Guests.** How long are guests allowed to stay? Where are they going to sleep? What rules will they follow?

9. **Sexile.** Can you sexile your roommate for the entire night? While you get busy in the room? What signal will you use?

10. **Bathroom.** If you have a bathroom in your room, how will you handle sharing it? What if your schedules overlap and you both need it at the same time? What's the maximum length for showers?

RULES

To Living Peacefully with Your Roommate

1

Create house rules and stick to them.

2

Share.

3

If you borrow something, return it in the same condition as when you borrowed it.

4

Be considerate.

5

Have short-term guests only.

6

Have roommate meetings twice a month.

7

Have roommate dinners or movie nights once a week.

8

Apologize if you do something inconsiderate.

9

Study together.

10

Don't gossip about your roommate.

Keeping Track of Your Roommate

Each of you should post your class, work, and practice schedules in a visible area so that everyone knows when the others are coming and going. That way you can schedule some private time in your room if you need it. But don't be shocked when your roommates don't stick to their schedules. Skipping classes and other commitments happens quite often—be understanding about your roommate's needs, and he/she wil be understanding about yours.

The Roommate from Hell

Sometimes a roommate can be a nightmare. If you're really having a problem with your roommate, don't hesitate to go to your resident assistant. Often, dorms will offer mediation, or even move you if it gets really bad. You didn't come to college to be abused, to feel demoralized, or to live in squalor. Report a problem if you're miserable. Realize that there will probably be times when you hate your roommate, and that's okay. Just don't follow through on those revenge fantasies. The feeling will most likely pass.

The RA

A resident assistant, also known as an RA, is another student—usually a junior, senior, or graduate student—who lives in the dorm and helps students with anything from personal problems to security issues and everything in between. RAs aren't paid: they exchange their time for free housing. Your RA should be the first person you go to when there's a problem. He/she will also schedule programs for your floor, usually a monthly food party, which is often the only way to get anyone to attend. The RA decorates the hallway, often sorts your mail, goes on rounds to make sure everything in the dorm is okay, and gives out candy or condoms. RAs should have an open-

Stopping Conflicts Before They Start

Schedule a 15-minute meeting with your roommate twice a month where you get together and talk about anything that's bothering you. Be open, but not critical. Try to come up with a compromise if there's a problem.

door policy, and you can go to them any time of the day or night.

The RA is probably not going to be your best buddy, and though he/she seems like a safe person to cling to, you're better off making first-year friends as soon as possible. Your RA is also probably not going to date you. Most dorms have policies against that, so look elsewhere for romance.

Dating in the Dorm

What do you do when you break up with someone and then have no choice but to see that person every day? What if he/she thinks you're dating because you've hooked up, but you just wanted a casual affair? Absolutely, positively do not rush into a relationship with someone in your dorm. Get to know the person before you add any more complications to an already-complicated year.

Hot or Not

The rumors of incredible sexual exploits in college are true at some schools. It's not unusual for a drunken threesome or foursome (or moresome) to occur. A fair amount of same-sex experimentation goes on as well.

Other campuses are conservative, and people often graduate (yes, *graduate*) without having so much as kissed anyone. Whatever you do, don't brag about any of this stuff. The whole dorm will know what you've done by dinnertime. And be safe!

Doing Laundry

Your dorm should have a laundry room. Every college student knows the importance of saving quarters, so get used to hoarding those precious, shiny coins. Put every quarter you have into a little sack designated for laundry—and then hide it! If your roommate knows where your quarters are, you won't have them when you've run out of underwear.

10 Tips for Cleaning Your Clothes

1. Separate your laundry into whites and darks. Some people do a middle-color wash, but do you have the energy and quarters for that? No.

2. Follow the instructions on the machine.

3. Add one cup of bleach to your whites: it does wonders.

4. Don't leave your laundry; instead, use that time to sit in the laundry room and study. If you leave, your clothes might leave too—without you.

5. Don't leave your clothes in the dryer for too long or they will age quickly and look faded.

6. Fold everything when you take it out of the dryer. If you wait until you trudge it up to your room, everything will be tragically wrinkled.

7. Check all of the labels on your clothing to make sure that everything is machine washable.

8. Hand wash delicate items. Most items that say "dry clean only" can actually be hand washed in cold water.

9. If you don't have time to iron, try using spray-on wrinkle remover: it really works.

10. Socks tend to disappear in the wash. No one knows where they go: it's one of those mysteries of life. If you want to keep all of your socks, wash and dry them in a mesh bag.

Do your own laundry and don't offer to do anyone else's. Taking your roommate up on an offer to do your laundry or offering to do his/hers because you're doing yours sets a bad precedent. Do your own dirty work. After a little practice, you'll soon figure out how not to end up with a load-full of pink socks and underwear.

4

CAMPUS LIFE

"When I first got to campus I thought I'd never find my way around. Now, it seems like a little village. You get to know everyone in your regular daily path."

Wendy B.
Michigan State University

In this chapter you'll get the scoop on all the on-campus resources and all the bureaucracy that goes along with being a college student. We'll also take a close look at how you can get the support you need to keep yourself emotionally and physically safe. Finally, we'll check out all the mind-expanding, fun stuff you'll have access to on campus.

The Basics

Upon arriving on campus, the first thing you need is a campus map to orient yourself with the basic layout of the place. You will receive a map during your first-year orientation, and you should carry it around with you at all times. If your school offers orientation tours of the campus, sign up.

It won't take you long to figure out where your dorm and the dining hall are: those are places you will visit countless times in your first days on campus. When you look at your map, highlight or circle all of the places that will be an integral part of your first-year experience, beginning with the library.

The Library

A college or university library is nothing like your hometown's quaint public library. The collections at college libraries are *large*, so large that the libraries often need to be separated by subject matter. If you're attending a large university, there may be a medical library, a law library, and a science library, in addition to the main library. The main library often holds millions of books.

If your college library doesn't have what you need, you can request an *interlibrary loan*. Basically, you put in an order for a book with your college library, and then another school mails your school the book. A librarian will walk you through the steps your first time.

Library Hours

Your college library is open much later than your local public library. Most college libraries stay open until at least 11 P.M. and stay open later during midterms and finals. Many libraries stay open 24 hours a day.

The Computer Center

The computer center (or computer lab) is the place on campus where banks of computers are set up for student use. If you don't have a computer, this is where you'll be spending a lot of your time. Even if you have your own computer, you'll still use the computer center on your way home from class to check email or when your computer crashes. Some computer centers have course-specific software loaded on them, which means you'll have to use these computers to complete your coursework.

Colleges usually have a computer or technology services office, where you can get help configuring your computer to your college intranet, troubleshoot any glitches on your machine, and attend crash courses on everything from academic web surfing and computer basics to HTML and basic programming.

You will not be permitted to leave your work on the computer center computers, so be sure to bring a floppy disk or CD to save your files. Most labs also have printers, but you may be charged a fee for each page you print.

The College Bookstore

College bookstores contain much more than just books. Finding your college bookstore won't be hard: if you see a display window with your school logo and mascot on everything behind the glass—sweaters, shirts, socks, jackets, posters, and mugs—then you've found it.

You'll be able to get some basic necessities at your college bookstore, like backpacks, floppy disks, CDs, extension cords, pens, printer paper, and so on. A word of warning: if you're on an isolated campus, the bookstore will be pricier than a discount store for these basics.

"The line at the bookstore is so long at the beginning of the semester, you need a backpack full of energy bars and some sports water just to make it to the register."

Lucy M.
Columbia University

The Copy Shop

Some of your professors will request that you go down to the campus copy shop to pick up course materials. These professors have decided to put together a course packet consisting of photocopies from various books. If they're only using a few pages from a book, they're saving you the expense of having to buy the whole thing. Simply tell the copy shop the course number and professor's name, and they'll be able to locate the proper course packet for you.

You'll be able to do your own photocopying and binding there as well. The campus copy shop is generally less expensive than those big corporate copy places.

The Writing Center

The writing center offers assistance to students who need help with their writing assignments, and the writing tutors there will do everything from helping you get started on a paper to revising specific parts. The tutors will *not* write your paper for you. Most of the tutors in the center are grad students or seniors majoring in English. They are trained to help you with writer's block, grammar, style, tone, and clarity.

The Tutoring Center

If you ever have trouble with your coursework, visit the tutor center. The tutors who work there are advanced undergraduate and graduate students who are experts in every discipline.

As with the writing center employees, tutors are not going to do your work for you. They're not there to write your papers or do your math problems: the tutoring center is for struggling students, not lazy ones. Tutors are there to make sure you know how to do your work so that you can pass your courses.

The tutoring center will be open during normal business hours. But since many tutors are students who live on campus, you may be able to arrange for private lessons with your tutor during off hours.

The Athletic Center

The athletic center or gym is a great on-campus asset, especially when the "freshman fifteen" creeps up. A college athletic center is much larger and has better equipment than a high school gym but is nowhere near as high-tech and fabulous as a membership gym.

Find out if your gym offers fitness and nutrition classes (most do). Gym hours vary from school to school, but they are generally open fairly late.

The Health Center

The scope of your school's health center—sometimes called the *infirmary*—will depend on the size of your school. Most schools offer basic health services as a part of your tuition. You will have access to mental health and crisis counselors and at least one nurse, as well as gynecologists and primary-care specialists. If you're attending a large university, your campus health center may be the size of a small hospital.

The Student Center

The student center (or student union) is the heart and soul of campus life. The student center is the place on campus to hang out with friends, study, have snacks, watch TV, and hold club events. Most campus clubs will meet at the student center, and many of the support centers for students will be housed there as well.

Residential Life Office

The folks at the residential life office take care of student housing on campus. They're the ones who set you up with roommates, who make sure you have the keys to your room, and who check that you haven't put holes in the walls. If you have a problem with your roommate or have a special housing need, these are the people who are going to help you out.

Ride Board

If you're looking for a ride home over Thanksgiving or winter break, check out the "ride board" in the student center. Students with cars post where they are driving to and what they'd like from you in return—usually just gas and toll money, which is a lot cheaper than taking a train or a plane.

The Registrar's Office

The registrar's office handles academic registration. It creates the academic calendar and schedules and handles all the official paperwork that leads you to graduation. The office also holds all your academic and personal records.

Do not wait until the last minute to visit the registrar's office during the class registration period. Classes are often meted out on a first-come, first-serve basis. If you don't choose fast, you'll wind up taking Intro to Basketweaving when you really needed Advanced Calculus.

The Bursar's Office

The bursar's office is all about the Benjamins: this is where you'll go to pay your tuition and fees. The bursar will set up a payment plan for your tuition if you don't have the cash on hand and will send you your loan and scholarship checks. If your parents are paying your tuition, they will get to know the people at the bursar's office quite well.

The Ombudsman

The term *ombudsman* originated in sixteenth-century Sweden and means "the representative or protector of the people." A campus ombudsman helps to resolve conflicts between students, faculty, and staff. The ombudsman also helps out when you feel you're up against an unfair administrator or professor. If you have a problem and you don't know what to do, the ombudsman is your campus superhero. The ombudsman, however, is not campus security. For emergencies, always contact the campus security or your RA.

The Financial Aid Office

The financial aid office has information on loans, grants, and scholarships. The employees will explain what your

Disability Support

The government requires schools to make accommodations for students with physical or learning disabilities. If you have a disability, contact your school before you arrive on campus to ensure that all the resources you need are available.

financial options are and help you find money for college. Check out the financial aid office even if you think you aren't eligible for financial assistance. You'll be surprised by the number of options available to you.

You'll receive your student loan checks through the bursar's office, not the financial aid office. Remember the difference between the two and you'll save yourself the trouble of standing in the wrong line in the wrong building.

Campus Clubs

Campus clubs connect students who have similar interests. If you are interested in joining a club on campus, or even starting one, head down to your student center for more information. There, you'll find a list of all the groups, as well as when and where they meet.

Academic Clubs

In high school, people often join academic clubs because they think it will look good on their college applications. In college, most students join academic clubs because they actually care about the subject matter.

Club members participate in community service, chat with alumni, have access to career development and networking seminars, and invite guest lecturers to speak on related topics.

Activist Clubs

College campuses generally welcome political activism. Activists groups organize students on campus in several ways: they get out the vote during election years, they stage protests and rallies on world events, and they serve as an outlet for community service. Political clubs bring in pundits, politicians, and experts to speak on a variety of current events. They also organize informal chats that

Fighting Prejudice

Contact an RA if you're facing discrimination in the dorms or your campus ombudsman if you feel there is any discrimination in a classroom setting. There should also be a university office (often called Minority Student Affairs) that helps minority students deal with racism, discrimination, and abuse.

10

POPULAR
Academic Clubs

1
Biology Club

2
English Lit Club

3
Media Studies Club

4
Economics Club

5
Accounting Club

6
Pre-Med Club

7
Pre-Law Club

8
Sigma Delta Pi
(Hispanic Honor Society)

9
Psi Chi
(Psychology Honor Society)

10
Lambda Pi Eta
(Communications Honor Society)

help students absorb what they're learning. Whether they push to the left, the right, or the center of the political spectrum, activist groups remind students that they are a part of the larger world.

Recreational Clubs

If you've got a hobby that you don't want to give up in college, or if there's an activity that you'd love to try for the first time, then a recreational club is the organization for you. Most colleges have tons of activities to choose from.

Try to get your feet moving at your school's swing dance club or learn Hapkido at the martial arts club. Do you like photography? Join the photo club. Are you a jazz aficionado? Start a jazz-lovers group. By nature, recreational clubs tend to be less political or community-service oriented. They tend to meet informally and often organize trips off campus.

Intramural Sports Clubs

If you have an interest in sports but no time to try out for a competitive team, you can stay healthy and meet like-minded folks through intramural athletic clubs on campus. Intramural teams don't just play the most popular sports, like baseball, basketball, football, hockey, and soccer (although you'll certainly find these sports clubs on most college campuses). You'll also find rugby, golf, tennis, softball, racquetball, fencing, and Ultimate Frisbee, among many others.

Community-Based Clubs

Community-based clubs serve a number of functions on campus. They support minority students who want to fight for social justice, they allow students from similar cultural backgrounds to celebrate their heritage, and they bring together diverse student populations to help strengthen the campus community by forming dialogues on important issues. Some community-based groups also support international students who might be dealing with a crisis in their home country.

Campus Events

Campus events are one-shot deals, once-in-a-lifetime chances to meet famous writers, pundits, professors, artists, politicians, business leaders, and musicians. To find out what's going on at your college, join a few campus listservs (internet listings) that interest you, check your email regularly, and glance over those flyers you see posted all over campus.

Readings

Whether you're a student of literature who loves poetry or a political science major who's closely followed the career of a pundit, you'll have an opportunity to get an insider's perspective from your favorite authors at on-campus readings. Campus readings also support budding writers and poets on campus. If you're an aspiring writer, you might want to get up and read some of your own work.

Lectures

"Before I got to college, a 'lecture' meant something I avoided from my parents."

Peter K.
Long Island University

People who give public lectures on campus are experts in their field and often come from other colleges to speak. At many public lectures you'll notice that your own professors are there taking notes and asking questions. College professors are lifelong students who must stay current on everything that goes on in their fields: new data, new methodologies, new technologies, and new ways of thinking about the world.

On campus you'll find lectures on politics, current events, the history of literature, business ethics, new discoveries in math and science, information on social movements, new biographical information about historical figures, and much more.

Charity

Part of being on a college campus is learning how to be a force for change in the world outside of school. There are many clubs and associations on campus that help organize fundraisers for charity. Joining a group of like-minded individuals to help promote a common cause helps connect you with the world off campus and lets you to forge new friendships.

Workshops

College campuses hold workshops on everything from speed reading to web design. Workshops can help you boost your grades, prepare for the job market, keep physically fit, or learn a craft. Sometimes, experts will stop by campus for limited engagements and hold workshops on their area of expertise. Some workshops cost additional money, but most of the time attendance is free with your student ID.

Discussion Groups

There are three types of discussion groups on campus: civic discussion groups, academic discussion groups, and personal discussion groups.

A civic discussion group focuses on a current world event and brainstorms solutions to world problems; some of these groups will require you to do outside reading. In an academic discussion group, students get together and read the works of an author or study one aspect of a discipline in order to discuss the larger role they play in academia. Personal discussion groups offer emotional support to students who are dealing with grief or depression, or students who have been the victim of racism or violence.

Art Openings and Film Screenings

Art openings and film screenings on campus showcase the work of celebrated artists, as well as student and faculty artists. Many large universities have state-of-the-art screening rooms and well-funded art museums; at these

Concerts

Campuses with concert halls will frequently hold public concerts featuring classical music, bands, and orchestras. Go and enjoy the sweet sounds of campus life. Or join a band, learn how to play an instrument, and get involved yourself.

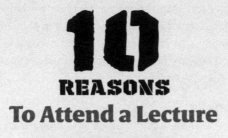

REASONS
To Attend a Lecture

1

Learn something new about a topic that interests you without the stress of tests or term papers.

2

Better understand some of the more difficult concepts in your discipline.

3

Impress your professors; they might even give you extra credit for attending.

4

Get more involved in a discipline, especially if you're planning on graduate studies.

5

Learn about a new field you'd like to major in.

6

Incorporate a lecturer's comments into a paper.

7

Meet other students who are interested in a certain topic or methodology.

8

Feel like a part of the academic community.

9

Meet famous writers and thinkers.

10

Get free food at the reception afterward.

schools, you'll be competing with members of the local community to get into an event.

If you are a student artist or filmmaker, working with an on-campus art organization offers valuable training and an opportunity to network with other artists and creative professionals.

Campus Rules

A college campus is a social microcosm. Every school has its own rules of interaction. If you want to get along with the other members of your community, start following these rules now.

Bias/Speech Codes

Almost all campuses have bias/speech codes that are strictly enforced. If you make statements that are perceived as racist, sexist, or homophobic, or if you attack the ethnicity or religion, of another student, a faculty member, or a staff person, you could be expelled. You can question ideas and ethics, but you can't threaten people with your words or actions.

Defending Yourself

Unfortunately, your school is not going to be a peaceful utopia: crime exists on college campuses. Find out where your school's campus security office is and carry the office phone number with you. Many schools have security phones set up around campus that will automatically put you through to a security officer.

You also have a right to defend yourself against verbal assaults and discrimination. Some universities have a student ethics office where you can report anything you find derogatory or sexually inappropriate.

10 Reasons to Go to the Ethics Office

1. You see another student cheating.
2. You know someone is plagiarizing.
3. You encounter a professor making a pass or hitting on a student.
4. You hear a professor or student make racist remarks.
5. You hear a professor or student make inappropriate sexual remarks.

6. You see someone stealing.
7. You believe that you are being graded unfairly because of your gender, religion, social class, ethnicity, political views, or sexual orientation.
8. You feel that someone in the university system isn't respecting your privacy.
9. You believe a health care practitioner at the university is behaving inappropriately.
10. You know someone is lying to deliberately harm someone else's reputation.

The Bottom Line

There is so much to do and see on a college campus. Almost every college student will discover a club, a sport, a craft, or a cause that satisfies her or his interests. And if on the off-chance you don't find an appealing outlet, you always have the power to start your own revolution. Do your own thing: devise your own organization if you've got the motivation and the passion. Build it and they will come.

5

SOCIAL LIFE

"Hear no evil, speak no evil——and you'll never be invited to a party."

Oscar Wilde

To Party or Not to Party

When you think *college*, do you think *party*? Toga parties, keggers, and really cheap booze are all part of the college experience. It's important to have fun while you're in school. After all, college is the ideal place to meet new people and create your own network of peers. But there's more to college than Bacchanalian bashes. You'll find all sorts of social events on campus that don't revolve around partying and getting drunk. For example:

1. Check out the clubs on campus. Even the Spelunking Club and the Chess Club have parties and events.

2. Activist groups on campus have a lot of social events, because they want to draw members.

3. Religious groups regularly hold social functions, and you don't have to practice the religion to attend.

4. The office of student life sponsors dances, coffee houses, picnics, films, concerts, student forums, and other events.

5. Fundraising events are common on campus. Volunteer to help and you'll find plenty of people to chat with.

6. The campus art museum is a good place to look for social events, including openings, lectures, and special guests.

7. Sporting events are very social—you will have a common bond with the people around you because everyone's rooting for the home team.

8. Joining the student government is a great way to meet people while making a difference on campus.

9. Event message boards advertise everything from karaoke nights to poetry readings.

10. Volunteering for the school paper, at the campus radio or television station, or at the yearbook will guarantee you a close network of people.

It can be a little intimidating to show up at events alone. That's precisely why schools sponsor so many events, especially at the beginning of the year. They want their first-year students to feel comfortable right away.

These events are designed for people who don't know one another. Before you know it, you'll find your social calendar so filled with events, you'll have trouble finding time to study. Which brings us to . . .

Finding a Balance

Life can't be all partying or all studying. Finding a balance is important to succeeding in your first year. If you tip the scales one way or the other, you're bound to become discouraged. Party all the time and you'll probably fail your classes and end up back at home. Study all the time and you'll miss one of the most important parts of college: making friends and socializing.

Due Dates

Imagine having a ten-page term paper due on Tuesday when it's Monday night and you've been hanging out with friends and socializing since last Thursday. Can you blow off the assignment? No. You're better off telling your new friends that you'll see them later, then hoofing it to the library to at least start your paper. On that fateful Monday night, you'll be glad to have three pages and an outline done. "That'll never happen to me," you say? *Sure* it won't. We wish you could hear the laughter emanating from generations of college grads. It happens to the best of us.

Imagine, again, that you've got that paper due and there's a great party going on across campus. Your crush is going to be there, as are all of your friends. If you had written the paper earlier, you could have gone to the party. Remember, your grades are part of your future. There will always be other parties.

Don't Cut Class

Guess what? Your professors don't care if you're tired, hungover, or otherwise incapacitated from partying hard. You have to go to class anyway. Skipping class because you've socialized too much is unacceptable, as is cutting class to do some socializing. You never know when you're *really* going to get sick or have something unexpected happen and have to skip class for a valid reason. Go to class first, party later.

Making Friends

Making friends is essential to surviving college. Your first few weeks can be lonely, but meeting new people will help to lift your spirits. The less alone you feel, the better you'll do in class and the more fun you'll have during your first year.

10 Great Ways to Make Friends

1. **Be yourself.** That's the best way to make friends. Remember, all the other first-year students are in the same boat as you.

2. **Warm up.** Don't play it cool because you think that people will respond to your mysterious nature. In reality, they'll be put off and won't bother approaching you.

3. **Hold a social hour.** Once you get to know your roommates, plan a social hour in your room and invite the other people on your floor. Offer simple stuff like cookies and soda. Nothing draws college students out of their rooms like free food and drinks.

4. **Eat together.** Find someone else in the cafeteria who's alone and ask if you can sit next to him/her. If you've found a group of people to eat with already, then ask someone who's sitting alone to join your group.

5. **Join clubs.** Go to some club "meet and greets." The first semester of the year is chock-full of social gatherings set up by groups on campus, and they are all thrilled to have extra attendees.

6. **Call on classmates.** Get phone numbers and email addresses from the people in your classes. If you're too shy to say it's because you're trying to make friends, tell them that you want their info so you can share notes or form a study group. Later, you can get in touch and ask them to join you in the cafeteria or at the movies.

7. **Form a study group.** Forming a study group is the perfect way to make friends. You don't have the pressure of asking others to do something socially, but it's easier to make friends once you've established a studying relationship.

8. **Get out of your room.** Seems obvious, doesn't it? But a lot of first years hole up in their rooms, content with television, textbooks, roommates, and mopey solitude. People aren't going to come to you. Get out there!

9. **Remember your roomies.** Your roommates can become your best friends if you cultivate a relationship with them. Plan party nights out and pizza nights in.

10. **Go Greek.** Joining a fraternity or sorority is like "instant friends, just add beer." If the frat life is for you, check out the scene on campus and explore a few of the organizations.

The Greek System

Most colleges have fraternity and sorority houses on campus. Collectively, these groups are called the "Greek system," because each house is named after two or three letters of the Greek alphabet. There are social Greek organizations, as well as those dedicated to a particular profession, such as medicine, law, engineering, or journalism.

A lot of what you've heard about fraternities and sororities is true. There are plenty of Animal House antics going on. But frats and sororities aren't just about all-night keggers and random hook-ups. Greek organizations do a lot of community service: they raise money for charities, volunteer in soup kitchens and for other community organizations, and organize food drives on campus. These events are great résumé builders, and employers see participation in Greek organizations as a plus. Among other things, it means that you have some measure of discipline and that you managed to maintain decent grades in college despite your extracurricular commitments.

10 Reasons to Go Greek

1. Lower drop-out rate than non-Greek students
2. Instant community, which is crucial during your first year
3. Leadership opportunities, which will serve you well later in life
4. Community service that will add credits to your résumé
5. Support structure, which helps students during hard times
6. Tutoring and academic support

10
IMPORTANT
Greek Terms

1 **Fraternity or Frat:** Greek organization for men

2 **Sorority:** Greek organization for women

3 **Rush:** The recruitment period at the beginning of the semester, when you are asked to join the organization

4 **Bid:** An invitation to join a frat or sorority

5 **Pledge:** A new recruit. You're not yet a full member of the organization, but you're one step closer to being accepted.

6 **Hazing:** Initiation rituals designed to perpetrate discomfort, pain, or embarrassment. Technically, hazing is illegal, but it is often done anyway.

7 **Initiation:** The formal ceremony inducting pledges into a frat or sorority

8 **Chapter:** The larger organization under which certain frats and sororities exist

9 **Intramural:** Sporting events between Greek organizations organized by the university

10 **Panhellenic Council:** The governing body for sororities

7. Parties, parties, parties
8. Intramural sports
9. Nice houses with great cooks
10. Networking opportunities after graduation

Of course, there are also reasons not to join a Greek organization. There are dues and fees, which can put quite a dent in your pocketbook. You also may not be the "frat type" and prefer to go it alone. Believe us, you'll be able to find friends even if you don't join a house. While it can be tough to be an independent on a campus that's mostly Greek, don't feel obligated to join.

Greek Parties

Yes, the parties are all they're cracked up to be. Some of them are legendary. But they can also be dangerous. Campuses that have had trouble with Greek parties in the past have put restrictions on the types of parties they can have, often banning alcohol from the houses, or making parties BYOB (bring your own beer/booze). Alcohol-related deaths, injuries, and sexual assaults are not uncommon at these parties, so it's no wonder why universities are concerned.

Parties are fun, no doubt. But getting so drunk that you vomit in public or are taken advantage of by someone isn't the kind of experience you should be looking for. Your only protection against the potential perils of frat parties is to stay sober.

10 Things About Frat Parties

1. If you're female: just smile and walk on in.
2. If you're male: check to make sure the party is open to outsiders. If not, it doesn't hurt to begin by making friends with the house members.
3. Guys: bring girls with you. Ladies: bring friends (there's safety in numbers!).
4. Dress for the party. Don't show up in a toga if it's a formal event. Walk in like you belong there.
5. Don't get drunk. Your boundaries will be blurred and you might do something you'll regret (or something that will earn you a black eye).

6. Bring something. If your hands are full of drinks or snacks, you're more likely to be welcomed.

7. Have fun at the party. Make yourself a valued part of the event.

8. Always have a plan of escape, unless you're ready to go fisticuffs with a whole houseful of drunk frat guys.

9. People who hang out at the frat houses all the time without joining are called *frat rats*. Don't go to a lot of their parties or spend the night in the house unless you plan on joining or dating one of the members.

10. If you don't want to drink too much or you're not sure how you handle alcohol, don't play drinking games. There are dozens of games geared toward getting drunk that often lead to complete incapacitation of the participants.

The Greek Alphabet

At some point during pledging you're going to have to memorize the Greek alphabet, and you'll probably have to recite it backwards. Here it is, in case you want to get a head start:

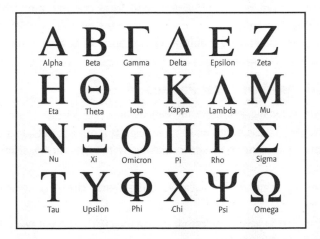

Drinking

While most first years aren't old enough to drink legally, alcohol invariably plays a big role in their lives. This is probably the first time in your life that no one will be peeking over your shoulder. You have few rules and you're on your own. So, you might want to try a lot of the things that your folks wouldn't allow while you were living with them.

Booze is easy to come by, even for underage students. Many school-sanctioned parties that are supposed to be "dry" will have alcohol. Keg parties are the norm, and it goes without saying that sporting events and booze go hand in hand.

There are many serious health risks related to drinking, including vomiting (and choking on it in your sleep), passing out, and blacking out. For first-year students who may not be experienced drinkers, the risks are even greater. Incidences of violence, date rape, accidents, and death all increase when college students drink alcohol.

The Bar Scene

Why are we addressing the bar scene in a book about first-year students, most of whom are presumably well under the drinking age? Well, because many first years easily acquire fake IDs and start drinking at hole-in-the-wall college hangouts pretty soon after the semester begins. Most students don't go to bars to hang out and do a little social drinking. The idea is to get plowed. It's not unusual to see people throwing up in the bathroom or outside the bar because they've had one too many. So-called college bars offer really cheap booze, parties, contests, freebees, and anything else they can do to get kids into the place.

Underage drinking is illegal. If caught serving minors, the bar owner gets in trouble, and the bartender will be fined or fired, plus the underage drinkers will be arrested. Imagine having to call your folks for bail money. But get-

Alcohol Poisoning and Drug Overdoses

An overdose of alcohol or drugs can be deadly. Signs include unconsciousness; shallow breathing (more than 10 seconds between breaths); and pale, blue, or cold and clammy skin.

Hangover Cure

You're thirsty, your head aches, and your breath smells like something died in your mouth. The good news is you can make yourself feel better drinking a lot of water and juice, taking an analgesic (like aspirin, ibuprofen, or acetaminophen) and some vitamins, and eating some fruit.

ting arrested for underage drinking is a cakewalk compared to getting arrested for drunk driving. And that's far preferable to getting into a car accident and injuring or killing yourself, your passengers, or someone else on the road. For your sake, use caution and your best judgment when it comes to drinking. Remember, a bar isn't a place to hang out—it's a place that's built for drinking, and drinking only. Sure, there might be a pool table and dartboard, but if those were the main attractions of the place, people would be ordering club sodas all night long.

Social Drinking

Social drinking means having a drink or two on occasion, over a meal or with friends. Around 46 percent of college students report being occasional drinkers. Social drinking might sound sophisticated and fun, but it, too, has its consequences.

According to the organization Mothers Against Drunk Drivers (MADD), each drink consumed by college students increases their risk of missing a class by 8 percent. So, if you have four drinks in an evening, you are 32 percent more likely to miss the next day's classes than if you hadn't had any drinks at all. The group also reports that having five drinks every time you go out will result in your GPA going down by half a grade. Pretty sobering statistics.

Binge Drinking

More than 42 percent of first-year students report that they regularly "binge drink." There are conflicting definitions as to what constitutes binge drinking. In the United States, the general definition is consuming more than five drinks in one "episode," which can mean an hour or a whole day, if you're a man, or consuming more than four drinks in an episode, if you're a woman. Other countries define binge drinking as having more than ten drinks in a

"There's no doubt that drinking is a big part of most people's college experience. Unfortunately, so is dealing with a hangover the morning after."

**Linda R.
American University**

"One reason I don't drink is because I want to know when I'm having a good time."

**Nancy A.
Princeton University**

day, and others still as having at least two bottles of wine. Whatever the case, it pretty much means that you're drinking to *excess*.

The National Institute on Alcohol Abuse and Alcoholism (NIAAA) Reports That:

1. Males tend to binge drink more than females.
2. Binge drinking is highest among white students.
3. Binge drinking is higher in the Northeast than in the South.
4. Thirty-one percent of students meet the criteria for alcohol dependence.
5. Participating in drinking games increases levels of drinking and drinking-related problems.
6. Students who engage in risky drinking may have blackouts (memory loss during periods of heavy drinking); fatal and nonfatal injuries, including falls, drowning, and automobile crashes; illness; missed classes; unprotected sex that could lead to sexually transmitted diseases or an unwanted pregnancy; bad grades and academic failure; an arrest record; accidental death; and death by suicide.
7. More than 600,000 students a year are assaulted or commit assault while binge drinking.
8. College students who drink to excess may miss opportunities to participate in the social, athletic, and cultural activities that are part of college life.
9. Belonging to a Greek house and participating in college athletics are associated with heavier drinking.
10. Many students who drink heavily do not perceive that they have a problem.

The average first-year college male has a little more than nine drinks per week, and the average first-year college female has about four. Binge drinking? It sure seems like it. More than 40 percent of college students say they did something they later regretted while drunk. It's better to stay clear-headed and not have to make any apologies than to call your friends the morning after to ask them what you did last night.

STATS
From MADD on Drinking in College

1   1,400 college students die each year from alcohol-related causes.

2   500,000 others are injured.

3   70,000 are sexually assaulted.

4   400,000 engage in unprotected sex.

5   College students spend about $5.5 billion on alcohol each year—more than they spend on books, soda, coffee, juice, and milk combined.

6   After the drinking age was changed to 21, researchers found that teenage deaths in fatal car crashes dropped considerably, in some cases up to 28 percent.

7   In 2001, more than half a million people were injured in alcohol-related car accidents—an average of one person injured every two minutes.

8   As a result of their drinking, about 25 percent of college students report academic consequences, 11 percent report damaged property, and 5 percent are involved with campus security or the police.

9   Students who attend schools with high rates of heavy drinking experience a greater number of secondhand effects, including disruption of sleep or studies; property damage; and verbal, physical, or sexual violence.

10   44 percent of college students report at least one symptom of alcohol abuse or dependency.

Drinking and Driving

Never, ever, *ever* drink and drive. Drunk driving is a serious crime. Nearly 30 percent of college students report drinking and driving: don't be one of them. One half of all fatal car accidents involving 18- to 23-year-olds are alcohol-related.

Confronting a Friend

It's pretty likely you'll encounter people who are frequently drunk during your first year. Perhaps your roommate is constantly coming home wasted. Or maybe your neighbor has started throwing Tuesday night keg parties that go well into Wednesday morning. Whatever the case, a person with a substance abuse problem can be a terror when he or she is in close proximity to you day in and day out.

10 Tips for Confronting a Friend

1. Wait to confront your friend until he or she is no longer drunk. You can't reason with people who have alcohol in their systems.
2. Ask the following questions. If your friend answers yes to any of them, there's a potential problem with alcohol:
   - Do you experience memory loss due to drinking?
   - Do you drink alone?
   - Do you get into trouble while drinking?
   - Do you lie about drinking?
   - Do you get drunk when you don't intend to?
   - Do you need to drink in order to relax?
   - Do you drink in the morning before school?
   - Do you drink when you get mad at someone?
   - Can you drink a lot more alcohol than someone else your size before feeling the effects?
   - Have your grades gone down?
3. Do not blame, accuse, or judge. This will only put your friend on the defensive.
4. Don't let your friend change the subject. He/she might turn the topic to your behavior. If that happens, bring the conversation back to alcohol abuse.

10
SIGNS
Of Alcohol Abuse

1   You need increasingly large amounts of alcohol to get drunk or feel the effects of the alcohol.

2   You experience withdrawal from alcohol.

3   You drink alcohol to relieve or avoid withdrawal symptoms.

4   You drink alcohol in larger amounts or over a longer period of time than usual.

5   You drink when you had planned not to drink.

6   You experience a persistent desire to control your drinking.

7   You make unsuccessful attempts to stop your drinking.

8   You spend a lot of time buying alcohol, using it, or recovering from its effects.

9   You give up on or are not as involved in social or recreational activities that don't center around alcohol use.

10 You continue drinking alcohol even though you know it's causing or worsening physical or psychological problems.

5. If you have taken care of your friend before when he/she was drunk, say you won't do it anymore. If you keep bailing your friend out of these messes, the problem might easily continue.

6. Don't get angry; be calm and compassionate. Realize that your friend will immediately become defensive. You're just there to state the facts and to listen.

7. Prepare for the talk by gathering some information on substance abuse. Alcoholics Anonymous has a lot of information available in the library or online.

8. Let your friend know that you will be supportive if he/she decides to get some help.

9. Invite your friend to do activities with you that don't involve alcohol.

10. You don't have to confront your friend alone. Go to your RA or someone at the health center at your school for some help. Getting people to realize they have a problem is often a huge job for the average person.

Treating Addiction

Most colleges have options available for treatment, including inpatient rehab, outpatient treatment centers, therapy, and 12-step groups. Don't be embarrassed about seeking help. It's far braver to face a problem than to deny it exists.

Drugs

According to the Department of Health and Human Services, the number of college students who use drugs has gone down significantly in recent years. That's not to say that drug use isn't prevalent on college campuses. At some schools, the number of students who abuse drugs is greater than 50 percent.

You've heard it a thousand times before, but it's definitely worth repeating: don't use drugs. College students who use drugs have more difficulty keeping their grades up than those who don't. And you will literally be putting your life at risk every time you get high.

10
WAYS
To Stay Safe

1 Tell a few people where you're going.

2 On a sheet of paper, write down where you're going and whom you're going with. Date it, and put it on your pillow before you leave.

3 Go with friends and don't lose them.

4 Leave with the same people you came with or with friends you planned to meet there.

5 Don't get so drunk that you're incapacitated.

6 Know how you're getting home. Have a backup plan in case your first plan falls through.

7 Never get in a car with someone who has had even one drink, and don't drive if you've been drinking.

8 Keep an eye on your friends to make sure they're okay. "Predators" often separate girls from the "herd" to assault them while they're drunk. Anyone can be a threat, even that cute guy from calculus class.

9 Never, ever leave a drink unattended. Also, don't accept a drink from anyone you don't know. If someone wants to get you a drink, go with them and watch it being poured.

10 Don't walk home alone at night.

Dating

Dating in college can be a lot of fun, especially for first years who are constantly meeting new people (which can equal many opportunities to hook up!). But don't forget that relationships are complicated. First-year students often become serial daters, skipping from partner to partner as a way of testing the dating waters. Here are a few tips to get you started and keep you out of dating hell:

10 Rules to Successful College Dating

1. If you're going to date someone in your dorm, do so with extreme caution and take things slowly. Gossip spreads fast.

2. Dating someone you meet in a class is ok as long as you start the relationship after midterms. If it turns ugly fast, you've only got a few weeks of seeing the person before class is over. If it's great, then you won't be distracted in class by your sweetheart for long.

3. Don't rush things. Go out on a few dates before you commit to anyone.

4. If you're going to be a player, you're going to land a player, as well as a bad reputation.

5. "No strings attached" relationships do not exist in college.

6. Having sex does not guarantee falling in love.

7. Lying is ugly; being yourself is much more attractive than pretending to be someone you're not.

8. If you really want to get to know someone, leave alcohol out of the dating experience. Yes, alcohol can help to break the ice, but it will also impair your judgment.

9. Lust is physical attraction. Love requires a more meaningful connection than just sex. It's easy to get these two emotions confused.

10. If you find yourself falling in love, don't be afraid to tell the other person: chances are he/she feels the same way about you.

"The only real valuable thing is intuition."

Albert Einstein

The Sweetie Back Home

Many first years are bummed about having to part with their high school sweethearts. Breaking up when you go to college doesn't mean you won't ever be together. It also doesn't mean that you have to rush into seeing someone else. It just means that you want to make the transition into college a little easier.

Sex

A study by the Centers for Disease Control and Prevention found that nearly 80 percent of students ages 18 to 24 are sexually active. We're not going to tell you not to have sex. We're not going to tell you to rush out and have it, either. For starters, it's not illegal if you're over 18. But there are some very serious, life-altering consequences to having sex, especially if you don't protect yourself.

10 Sex Risks

1. Between 20 and 25 percent of college students have been infected with a sexually transmitted disease (STD). So if there are 100 people at a party, 20 to 25 of them may have had or currently have an STD.
2. Condoms aren't 100 percent effective against pregnancy and disease, but if you're going to have sex, you should *always* use one.
3. Twenty percent of all people diagnosed with HIV are in their twenties.
4. One in five Americans has genital herpes, though 80 percent of those infected don't know it.
5. Herpes can be transmitted during oral sex.
6. The "pulling out" method is not safe: pregnancy and STDs can still occur.
7. Used alone, spermicidal agents have the highest failure rate among contraceptives.
8. Two-thirds of Hepatitis B infections are transmitted through sex.
9. Most people with an STD have no symptoms, so you can't tell if someone you're with has a disease or if you've contracted one.
10. By the time the symptoms of an STD appear, you may have already transmitted the disease to someone else.

We're not trying to scare you: we're just telling you the facts. If you want to avoid the risk of contracting an STD or getting pregnant, don't have sex. If you're going to have sex, always carry condoms with you, and have extras in case one breaks.

Sexual Assault

Sexual assault happens on most college campuses. Date rape is an all-too-common occurrence in college, especially among first-year female students.

If a person forces you to have sex, even if you know that person, you are the victim of rape. *No* is a complete sentence. If you can't say *no* or *yes* because you've passed out, it's not an automatic yes. No one should be having sex with you when you're unconscious. When you say no, you don't have to offer a reason for not wanting to have sex. You do not owe sex to anyone for any reason.

Here are some things you should know about sexual assault, as well as some ways to protect yourself from it:

1. Staying sober is your best defense against sexual assault.
2. Trust your intuition: if you feel uncomfortable in a situation, there's probably a good reason for it.
3. Use the buddy system at parties. Stay with your friends and keep an eye on each other.
4. Don't allow yourself to become isolated at a party with someone you don't know very well or someone you don't have reason to trust.
5. If a party becomes sexually charged, get out *immediately*.
6. If you do drink, watch your drink at all times and don't accept drinks from strangers or people you don't know well. It's easy to slip a "date rape" drug into any type of beverage.
7. Being drunk doesn't excuse someone's sexual aggression.
8. Date rape is a reportable crime. Take responsibility for yourself and report any wrongdoing: you could be saving someone from the same fate.
9. If he just met you, he doesn't love you. He doesn't *know* you! Use your common sense and keep yourself from being fooled into a situation you can't handle.
10. Yes, sexual assault *can* happen to you. Statistics show that it will probably happen to someone you know.

Peer Pressure

Come on, everyone's doing it! You want us to like you, don't you?

Be very suspicious of someone who tries to get you to do something you think is dangerous or questionable. There's a reason why you think the way you do, and it has nothing to do with being afraid. The person who's trying to peer-pressure you is the one who's actually afraid. This person wants company in his/her little mission. Whether it's alcohol, sex, or drugs, people who are pressuring you care about themselves, not about making you cool and having you "fit in." Before you give in to peer pressure, think about who is doing the pressuring and what their motives are.

Spring Break

Spring break conjures images of tanned bodies in bikinis, drinks with little umbrellas in them, and a week of frolicking in the clear blue sea. Sure, that's part of it. But the other side of the spring break is the 40 percent of college students who will drink till they pass out, the more than 2,000 of them who will be arrested, the dozens who will be the victims of date rape, and the handful who will die. Some vacation.

Again, the culprit here is alcohol, with its sidekicks drugs and peer pressure along for the ride. Spring break can be a lot of fun if you're careful. Don't get sloppy drunk, and use common sense.

The Bottom Line

Sorry we had to be such a bummer in this chapter. But we're only trying to scare the bejesus out of you because we care about you. We figure you'll find all the information you need on where to find the best parties and how to become a slacker when you get to college. What's important is that you strike a balance between having a good time and doing well in school. We'd rather you be safe, get good grades, and have a great college experience than end up in trouble because you didn't know your limits.

HEALTH

"A person too busy to take care of his health is like a mechanic too busy to take care of his tools."

Spanish Proverb

10

Health Center Services

1

Routine physicals

2

Immunizations

3

Allergy injections

4

Classes for quitting smoking

5

Weight control classes/nutritional counseling

6

Fitness tests

7

Massage/physical therapy

8

Pharmacy services

9

Birth control counseling

10

Counseling and psychological services

When you're sick, there's nothing better than staying home from school to watch mind-numbing daytime television, sip chicken soup under a warm quilt, and drink big spoonfuls of unbearably strong cough syrup. But the days of Mom and Dad bringing you glasses of orange juice and chewable vitamin C tabs are over.

In college, staying home from school means sitting in your room all day long while everyone else is out and about having fun. Don't expect your parents to show up at your dorm ready to take care of you. The good news is your school has plenty of provisions for you if you become ill or depressed, so you're not going it on your own.

The Health Center

Every college campus has a health center. If you're a full-time student, you'll be charged a health center fee, which allows you to use the facilities whenever you need them. The health center staff knows how to deal with illnesses that often plague college students, such as strep throat, the flu, and mono.

Some university health centers charge a small fee each time you visit, which is often waived if you make an appointment. If your health center can't provide you with a service you need, such as dermatology, they will generally refer you to a provider who works with the school's insurance program.

Your file in the university health center is absolutely confidential. The staff will not share it with your parents, professors, the government, or anyone else. Be completely honest with the doctors and nurses so you can get the proper treatment.

After-Hours Emergencies

If you have an emergency when the health center is closed, you should call 911. Some schools have special after-hours numbers for less serious medical problems that still need immediate attention. However don't hesitate to call 911 if you're worried about your health, because a condition you think can wait till morning might actually be very serious.

10
THINGS
That Go Around

No matter how hard you try to avoid it, you'll probably get sick at some point during your first year. The flu can immobilize an entire dorm for a few weeks. But if you take care of yourself, you'll recover from these illnesses quickly, with the least possible damage to your health and your schoolwork. Here are 10 common college maladies you may encounter:

1
The common cold

2
Strep throat

3
Bronchitis

4
The flu

5
Mononucleosis (mono)

6
Pneumonia

7
Urinary tract infection

8
Ear infections

9
Anemia

10
Sexually transmitted diseases (STDs)

10 Reasons to Call 911

1. Unconsciousness/fainting
2. Profuse bleeding
3. Broken bones
4. Eye injuries
5. Severe and persistent vomiting
6. Head trauma
7. Drug overdose
8. Chest pain
9. Dizziness/weakness
10. Severe difficulty breathing

Vaccinations

Most colleges require that you've had the MMR (measles, mumps, and rubella) vaccine. Recently, colleges have started requiring their first years to get the meningococcal meningitis vaccination, especially if they are living in residence halls, where close contact can spread this illness. You may also have to show proof of having received a tetanus, polio, or diphtheria vaccine.

Mental Health

Transitioning into a new life can be tough for many students. Every experience and interaction you have during your first year of college will be a new one, which means you'll have to find new ways of dealing with stress and feeling down. Fortunately, your school's mental health center can help you get through this tough time by offering counseling. Don't hesitate to use this service if you're feeling stressed, depressed, or confused: ignoring your mental health is just as bad as ignoring your physical health.

Counseling

Going to therapy or counseling to talk about your feelings doesn't make you crazy or unstable. In fact, it means just the opposite. Students who talk about their feelings feel balanced and are more likely to succeed in college than those who white-knuckle it.

The counselors who work at the mental health center are trained professionals who specialize in the mental health issues that frequently come up for college students. If your school offers graduate studies in psychology, the counselor may be a PhD student doing his or her internship. Don't worry, they're not just practicing on you: these people are already thoroughly trained to counsel people and are just logging hours toward their graduation or accreditation.

Group Therapy

Along with individual counseling, you can also join a group focused on a particular topic, such as grief, trauma, self-esteem, or eating disorders. People often hesitate to join a group therapy session, because it can be difficult sharing your emotions with a room full of strangers. But the members of the group are all there to work through their feelings, not to judge you, and it helps to see that other people are dealing with the same problems you're experiencing.

Depression

Depression is like a bad or sad mood that you can't snap out of. If it lasts for an extended period of time, depression becomes a serious medical condition and should be treated by a mental health professional. Everyone gets depressed at some time or another, but clinical depression is the type that doesn't lift. About 10 percent of all college students are diagnosed with clinical depression.

10 Signs of Depression

1. Feeling unrested and unable to get out of bed in the morning
2. Waking frequently during the night after nightmares/disturbing dreams
3. Ceasing to do things you once enjoyed
4. Difficulty concentrating
5. Drastic weight gain or loss
6. Frequent upsetting thoughts/worrying too much
7. Becoming emotional or upset for no obvious reason

8. Irritability/short temper
9. Feeling "slowed down"
10. Losing interest in life/suicidal thoughts and feelings

A lot of factors can trigger depression, including stress, new responsibilities, changes in your social life, and substance abuse. If you think you're depressed, contact your school's mental health center right away. Clinical depression does not go away on its own.

Taking Control

There are times when depression grabs hold so strongly that it feels impossible to shake. When things feel out of control, you have to find a way to regain your balance and work through your emotions. Before you do anything drastic, try one of the following coping methods:

1. Stop what you're doing and breathe.
2. Call your school's mental wellness center and make an appointment. Taking this first step helps you feel that you're taking control of your emotions, instead of allowing your emotions to take control over you.
3. Call your family. If you have loving support from your family, a phone call home may help alleviate some negative feelings.
4. Call a friend. If you have a supportive friend, tell him or her how you're feeling.
5. Write about your feelings. A journal doesn't judge or give advice. Sometimes just getting all of the negative thoughts down on paper helps.
6. Eat something starchy and fatty. Rich foods can calm you down and can give you a sense of ease.
7. Get some rest. Exhaustion might be adding to your bad mood.
8. Cry it out. There's nothing wrong with feeling sad and angry and just crying your eyes out. Sometimes "letting go" is the best remedy.
9. Find your RA and tell him/her you need help.
10. Think about what you really want. As hopeless as everything may seem, what you really need is a break from what's going on around you.

Suicide

Each year, 10,000 university students attempt suicide, and 10 percent succeed. These are frightening statistics.

Suicide happens when pain (emotional or physical) outweighs the resources a person has to deal with it. Suicidal feelings tend to dissipate when the person takes some action to relieve the pain, such as counseling. No one is going to think you're crazy for having suicidal thoughts, and there are people who can help you overcome these feelings. Most people who attempt suicide don't want to die but rather just want to be rid of the pain they're feeling.

If you're thinking of suicide, *immediately* stop whatever you're doing and tell someone. Call a suicide hotline or go to your school's mental health center, where you can talk to trained people who will help you deal with your thoughts and feelings. You're not alone.

Addiction

Substance abuse is pretty widespread among college kids, many of whom are either experimenting for the first time or continuing their drug and alcohol abuse but now with the added freedom of being away from home. Fifty-five percent of college students admit to using drugs, and even greater numbers admit to drinking alcohol regularly.

Alcohol is everywhere in college: at parties, sporting events, and even your dorm. Fifty percent of college males and nearly 40 percent of college females say that they binge drink. Thirty-one percent become alcohol abusers, but of those only 6 percent seek treatment while in college.

Alcohol can be deadly in large doses or when it's combined with other drugs. It's very likely that someone on your campus will die this year as a result of a drug overdose or alcohol poisoning. Don't let yourself become a statistic. If you or someone you know has an alcohol or drug problem, contact the mental wellness center at your college. They have resources to deal with addiction.

Homesickness

Homesickness afflicts most first-year college students and is especially common in the first few weeks of school. You've moved away from home for the first time and have left everything familiar and comforting behind.

You'll miss your friends, your pets, your room—you'll even miss your little brother's whining and your parents' nagging.

You can't avoid homesickness, but you can keep it from crippling you in college.

10 Ways to Curb Homesickness

1. Put up some favorite photos of your family and friends.

2. Make friends in your dorm. You can commiserate about your homesickness, and you'll be less lonely.

3. Email some friends back home. Don't make lengthy phone calls—it'll make you feel even more homesick and it will cost a fortune.

4. Write down 10 things you miss about home and 10 things you love about your new life in college.

5. Don't mope. Get out and do something fun.

6. Do something nice for yourself, like getting a massage, and don't feel guilty about it.

7. Call your family just to say hello. Don't throw a one-person pity-party on the phone. You'll feel better when you hang up if you didn't spend the time whining about how much you miss your cat.

8. Do your laundry. Getting busy and productive keeps your mind occupied on other things.

9. If your homesickness gets really bad, call your school's mental health center and make an appointment. Your feelings are valid and are worth talking out with a professional.

10. Don't rush home until vacation time (unless you live reasonably close to campus and can make a day trip). While you're home, the other people in your dorm will be getting to know one another well, and you'll miss out on all of that bonding.

"I didn't think I'd ever be homesick. I thought I'd be partying and living it up. Well, after two weeks I really missed home cooking and my own bed."

**Stephen O.
Marymount College**

Stress

Moving is one of the most stressful times in a person's life. When you move to college, you have the added burden of being on your own for the first time, making new friends, taking care of yourself, and starting a rigorous class schedule. All these factors make your first few months at college pretty stressful.

Stress affects both your mind and your body. It is a reaction to events happening in your environment, and can also be a reaction to something happening in your body (such as illness or hormonal changes). Most people can handle a certain amount of stress and can even use it to motivate them—for example, using the deadline for turning in a term paper as a stimulus for getting it done. But at some point the stress can become too much, and you may become overwhelmed and unable to handle everything that's going on.

If your world feels like it's falling apart, call the mental health center right away. Chances are nothing's really falling apart, and if something is, there is a resource at school to help you put it back together.

Stress Management

You won't be able to get rid of most of the stressors that come with college life, but you can choose to deal with them differently, which will reduce your stress level.

10 Ways to Handle Stress

1. **Relax.** Take thirty minutes for yourself each day to do something that requires as little effort as possible and doesn't use any brain power. Watch TV, read a trashy novel, people-watch—do whatever it takes, just as long as what you're doing is relaxing. Don't play video games, answer emails, or do anything else

that raises your heart rate and requires a lot of concentration. The idea is to become a cauliflower for the moment.

2. **Balance your workload.** Perhaps you've taken on too much. Write down all of your weekly obligations. Where is there time for you? Try to carve a couple of hours out of your day for "me time." You may have to give up an activity or obligation to do that.

3. **Get a massage.** Some universities offer massage at their health center. Call to find out. If not, perhaps you and a friend can swap massages.

4. **Meditate.** When you're going a hundred miles a minute, meditation is an opportunity to slow down for a while and reconnect with yourself. Meditation classes are often offered on campus.

5. **Sleep.** If you're tense, you may not be getting enough sleep. Aim for as close to eight hours a night as possible. If you lose too much sleep you can become ill and confused, and you won't perform well in school.

6. **Nap.** Can't get eight hours of sleep? Taking a twenty-minute nap during the day is refreshing. But don't nap for longer, because you'll wake up groggy and won't be able to sleep at night.

7. **Find your purpose.** We admit this is a tough one. But wandering aimlessly, not knowing what you're doing on earth, is even more difficult. Of course, finding your purpose is a lifelong journey, and nobody expects you to figure it out by the time you finish reading this chapter. So try to figure out what your purpose is for today. What are you doing to make your life better today? What are you doing to make someone else's life better today? What one thing can you do today to make yourself feel less stressed? How about finishing that chapter for physics class or cleaning your side of the room?

8. **Stop procrastinating.** Putting things off for later can cause extreme stress, especially as deadlines approach.

9. **Take a day trip.** Taking a day to get off campus to go hiking or camping can put you in a totally different frame of mind by the time you get back.

10. **Work out.** Yes, you're busy with all of the pressures of your new life, but you've got to make some time for regular exercise. Regular exercise helps the body to release the tension built up from too much stress and will help to regulate your sleep patterns and your appetite.

10

SYMPTOMS
Of Stress

1

Muscle tension

2

Chronic colds or other illnesses

3

Indigestion

4

Difficulty sleeping/fatigue

5

Headaches/backaches

6

Irritability/mood swings

7

Depression

8

Fear/anxiety/worry

9

Feeling overwhelmed

10

Forgetfulness/difficulty concentrating

Sleep

Stress and depression can lead to sleep disturbances. Either people can't fall asleep at all, or they'll hunker down under the covers all day, avoiding the world around them. Getting some balance in your life should help you find a normal sleep pattern. Eat right, exercise, deal with your feelings, and try not to procrastinate. Get to bed at a reasonable hour and get up about eight hours later.

If you have difficulty sleeping, make your bed as comfortable as possible with soft sheets and a cushy mattress topper. Use a small white-noise machine if background noises bother you. Ask your roommate to respect your sleeping schedule. If insomnia persists, make an appointment at the health center. Don't read in bed to fall asleep: you'll only train your brain to become sleepy when you read, which is not a good plan for a college student.

If you can't get out of bed and are sleeping more than ten hours a day, try to root out the cause. Are you *depressed*? Are you eating too much junk and sugar? Once you discover why you can't get out from under the covers, you can begin to solve the problem. Sleeping your college years away isn't going to make life any less stressful.

Sexual Health

College is often a time for hooking up and getting down. You're an adult now, and you can do what you want. But that doesn't mean that you can do what you want *indiscriminately*.

The most important rule of sexual health is a very simple one to follow: protect yourself. This doesn't mean just carrying condoms or being on the pill. This means not getting so drunk that you don't know what you're doing. It means knowing the person you're hooking up with and knowing what your boundaries are and how to enforce them. *No* is a complete sentence. So is *We have to use a condom.*

10

HEALTHY CHOICES
At a Fast Food Restaurant

1

Salad with low-fat dressing

2

Plain baked potato

3

Mashed potatoes

4

Any vegetable

5

Bean/vegetable burrito

6

Chicken burrito

7

Grilled chicken without mayo

8

Veggie burger

9

Skinless chicken

10

Turkey sandwich on whole wheat bread

STDs

Between 20 and 25 percent of college students will be infected with a sexually transmitted disease (STD). There are some nasty bugs out there that you definitely want to avoid, such as chlamydia, gonorrhea, syphilis, human papillomavirus, herpes, hepatitis B, and bacterial vaginosis. Some of these illnesses can be treated with antibiotics, while others, like herpes, are viruses that will be with you forever.

HIV/AIDS

One in every 500 college students is HIV positive. HIV is a potentially fatal virus that can be transmitted through sexual contact and causes the AIDS syndrome. When someone is infected, they may be symptom-free for many years and not even realize they are HIV positive. You can't tell by looking at someone if they have HIV. To protect yourself, always use a condom when you have sex. Be smart and don't put yourself at risk, no matter what your partner says.

If you're sexually active, get an HIV test regularly and make sure your partners have been tested recently. HIV tests are easy, confidential, and can save your life. There's no excuse not to get one.

Pregnancy

More than 31 percent of college students report that they've been pregnant or have gotten someone pregnant. Your health center should be able to provide you with birth control options, or you can always use the best form of birth control—the word *no*.

Eating Right

An important part of maintaining your health is eating well. Once you're in college, there won't be anyone around telling you to eat your veggies. You can have ice cream for breakfast, gummy bears for lunch, and cherry pie for dinner if you like. Who's stopping you? But we can guarantee that if you regularly eat like this you won't function the way you're supposed to and you'll put yourself at risk for getting sick. Furthermore, an unhealthy lifestyle promotes poor grades. Can what you eat affect your performance in school? Absolutely. Becoming conscious of your eating habits will help to keep you on top of your game.

EASY WAYS
To Eat Healthier

1   Don't skip breakfast. Your metabolism will slow down and you'll gain more weight.

2   Don't skip lunch. You'll overeat at dinner if you're famished.

3   Have at least two pieces of fruit a day, such as an apple and a banana.

4   Include at least two servings of vegetables a day (the slice of tomato and wimpy leaf of lettuce on your burger doesn't count).

5   When you eat bread and other starches, try to eat whole wheat or whole grain.

6   Cut out or drink less regular soda. One can of regular soda has 150 calories.

7   Cut out or drink less alcohol. Hard liquor has 70 calories an ounce, a can of beer has about 150 calories, and a glass of wine has about 200 calories.

8   Choose healthier snacks, such as air-popped popcorn and low-fat frozen yogurt instead of chips and ice cream.

9   Try to be good about what you eat during the week, then pig out on anything you want on weekends. That way you won't feel deprived.

10 Don't diet. Dieting makes you cranky and your performance in school will suffer. Instead, make a few changes to how and what you eat instead of how much you eat.

The Freshman Fifteen

Many first-year students gain fifteen to twenty pounds during their first semester. When you first get to school, look around your classrooms and note the svelte bodies of the students around you. By semester's end, most of them are going to be significantly bulkier. It could even happen to you.

What's the reason for the "freshman fifteen" phenomenon? In part, it has to do with the food choices offered to college kids in the dining halls. Fats and starches abound. Pizza, hamburgers, and french fries become the staple diet. Breakfast is generally sugary, and snacks tend to be fatty and salty. The perfect recipe for that "spare tire." College kids also don't have a lot of money to spend, and fast food is cheap and tasty. Most fast food pretty much equals fat food.

The weight gain also comes from the extra calories in alcohol. The first year of college is when most people are first exposed to the all-you-can-drink-mentality, and they overindulge. Aside from the many other side effects that alcohol causes, it causes tremendous weight gain. Alcohol also acts as an appetizer, meaning that it makes you hungry.

Better Food Choices

You can eat a lot as long as you're choosing the right foods. College is a stressful time, and a stressed body needs additional calories to function. But the body will cease to function well when those calories don't come with the nutrients the body needs to keep everything running in good order.

We don't have to tell you that a salad is healthier than a cheeseburger or that a baked potato is healthier than fries. But a cheeseburger tastes better, doesn't it? That's because it has a lot more fat in it than a salad does, and fat makes the body feel full and satisfied. But you can eat a lot more salad, veggies, and fruit and consume fewer calories than you would if you ate a greasy burger. More food equals a full belly. You don't need that junk food to feel satisfied.

10

Quick and Healthy Snacks

1

Bananas

2

Unsalted pretzels

3

Apples

4

Hardboiled eggs

5

Milk (dairy or soy)

6

Roasted soy beans

7

Raisins

8

Protein bars

9

Part-skim mozzarella string cheese

10

Yogurt

Grabbing and Going

Part of the reason first years gain weight is because they are always eating on the run. There's never enough time in the day for a sit-down meal. A doughnut and a can of soda are quick, but they don't constitute a healthy breakfast.

Try to have at least one meal a day while sitting at a table. Eating over the sink or on your way to class isn't great for the digestion. Eating more slowly helps you to eat less, which helps you maintain a normal weight. There's a mechanism in your brain that tells you when you're full. Unfortunately, the mechanism isn't triggered the second you get full. You can keep eating for a while before the stomach tells the brain to stop. If you eat more slowly, you give the stomach time to tell the brain that you don't need to eat anymore.

If you have to "grab and go," make better choices about what you're grabbing. Plenty of things besides fast foods are easy to take along with you. Also, keep something healthy in your backpack at all times. You're more likely to overeat unhealthy foods if you're starving because you've waited too long between meals.

Social Eating

Just about every event you attend in college will be focused on food and drinks. Parties have bowls of chips and seemingly limitless kegs. Your dorm will throw pizza parties and ice cream socials. If you rush a frat or sorority, each meeting will involve snacks or a meal. You'll order pizza with your roommates and have movie rental night, complete with candy and ice cream. Temptation is everywhere.

We're not going to tell you not to eat anything at these events. But you can control how much you eat. First, eat something healthy and filling before you attend an event. Next, drink a big glass of water right before you get there. Water helps you feel full and you're less likely to overeat.

"Everyone I know gained weight their first year. It happens. But most everyone takes it off in sophomore year. You get used to the food eventually and start really wanting salad."

**Lincoln A.
Rhodes University**

Finally, eat only a predetermined number of items and stick to that number. For example, decide before you get to the pizza party that you're only going to have one or two slices of pizza and one soda. If you're good at sticking to a plan, then you're set. If not, you may start to tip the scales. Don't say we didn't warn you.

Eating Disorders

Eating disorders can appear in the first year of college. Stress, school pressure, and homesickness can trigger eating too much—called bingeing—to comfort sad and lonely feelings. Eating too little, which is a symptom of anorexia, can bring a feeling of control to a stressed-out student, as can purging, which is a symptom of bulimia. But these disorders cause more harm than they do comfort. In the long run, eating disorders create serious health problems and lead to thousands of deaths each year.

Don't get caught in the dangerous cycle of eating disorders. If you think you have a problem, contact your health center right away. Because eating disorders are so common on college campuses, schools have professionals who know exactly how to deal with them. No one is going to judge you.

Eating While Studying

Studying can be pretty boring, and snacking helps to keep you awake and alert, which will keep you at the books longer. But snacking like this can also pack on the pounds if you're eating the wrong things.

If you choose your study snacks wisely, you can mindlessly eat as much as you want. The following foods have so much fiber and/or water content, it's nearly impossible to overeat them:

10 Eat-as-Much-as-You-Want Study Snacks

1. Grapes
2. Sliced bananas
3. Carrot sticks
4. Celery sticks
5. Plain rice cakes
6. Air-popped popcorn
7. Dried peas
8. Orange slices
9. Puffed wheat/rice/kashi/millet
10. Baked chips

Finding Your Groove

You don't have to be a health nut to keep yourself in good shape during your first year. Just use some common sense and do everything in moderation. Take it easy on yourself this year. You'll burn out if you do too much too soon. Find your own groove and ride it all year long.

You know yourself better than anyone around you. Listen to your body, your feelings, and your intuition, and you'll get through the year in stride.

7
MONEY

"Recommend virtue to your children;
it alone, not money, can make them
happy. I speak from experience."

Ludwig van Beethoven

Ah, now we're getting to the meat of things: money. All college students need it, and there's never really enough, unless you're the Olsen twins. Fortunately, you don't really need a ton of extra cash while you're in school. As long as you've figured out a way to cover the basic college costs—tuition, fees, housing (which often comes with a meal plan), books, equipment, and transportation home—you really only need some pocket cash.

Expenses

The key is figuring out how much extra cash will get you through the school year. You'll want some cash for movies, pizza, dates, music, clothes, and dorm room decorations. Depending on where you live (and *how* you live), your personal out-of-pocket expenses can range from $2,000 to $4,000 a year.

Where, exactly, is that money going to come from? Many students rely on their folks to pay their student loans while in college, but there are also scholarships, grants, internships, and work-study opportunities that you can get for yourself to help with expenses.

No matter how good you are about making or saving money, you'll find yourself short on funds at some point. That's OK, because college is the one time in your life where you can be really poor and still revel in it. Enjoy this time in your life, because after college it's not as cool to have holes in your socks. This chapter gives you some tips and tricks to acquire and save some cash in your first year of school.

Budgeting

Budgeting for what you *want* versus what you *need* is tricky. The only things you really need are food, clothing, and shelter. If you've brought enough weather-appropriate clothing with you, and if your dorm and meal plan are paid for in advance, then you shouldn't need a dime, right?

Oh, if only that were only true! For starters, you'll have to stock up on essentials, like school supplies. And you'll need a budget for personal expenses as well.

It's important to distinguish between needs and wants. When you're contemplating buying something, ask yourself if you really need it. Then ask yourself if you can get it cheaper somewhere else, like online. When using the phone, ask yourself if you need to call someone at peak hours or if the call can wait till later.

Below, we'll summarize some of the expenses you're likely to incur during your first year. There are two types of expenses you'll need to budget for: educational and personal. While our lists aren't exhaustive, they'll definitely get you thinking about what you'll need to survive college.

Educational Expenses

Educational expenses include school supplies, computer accessories, and books, which will be your biggest expense in this category.

Top 10 Educational Expenses

1. **Computer.** Most students bring a computer with them from home. Don't sweat it if you can't: the computer labs on campus should be open 24/7 (or at least late into the night). If you're buying a new computer, consider getting a laptop, which will run you anywhere from $600 to $3,000. Some computer companies give educational discounts to students.

2. **Printer.** This purchase falls somewhere in between the *want* and *need* categories, because you can burn your files onto a CD or email them to yourself and then print them in the computer lab. But should you

Impulse Shopping

We've all felt the thrilling need to buy something the instant we see it. Whenever you get that feeling, step away for a moment and ask yourself, "Is this something I really need?" Generally, people aren't impulsive about the things they need; it's the things they want that get their hearts racing and impair their judgment.

Used Books

You can save hundreds of dollars by purchasing used textbooks online. Visit **www.bn.com** and click on **New & Used Textbooks.**

want to buy a printer, add $70 to $300 to your budget. Add another $70 to $150 for extra ink cartridges.

3. **Books.** You'll end up spending $500 to $750 a year on books, depending on how many used books you can acquire.

4. **Writing supplies.** You'll need about $50 for pens, highlighters, pencils, and so on.

5. **Paper.** Add $75 for paper, notebooks, etc.

6. **Backpack.** Depending on how fancy you want to get, add $30 to $150 for a backpack or messenger bag.

7. **Calculator.** Add $5 to $50, depending on what kind of calculator you need.

8. **PDA.** You don't need one, but they're great to have and make life a lot easier. Add $99 to $600 to your budget. If you don't get a PDA, a cheap pocket calendar will do.

9. **Miscellaneous supplies.** This category includes portfolios, files, folders, binders, computer software, and just about anything else you can think of. Add about $250 to $400.

10. **mp3 player.** OK, you don't *need* one for college, but you can buy a handy recorder attachment that makes taking notes and recording ideas very convenient. You can also download books and listen to them on the fly. How's that for making the most of your time? Add $200 to $400.

You can't get out of many of these expenses, but you can shop wisely by waiting for sales, looking for bargains, and buying used items. Online auction sites are great for finding stuff on the cheap.

Personal Expenses

Personal expenses vary depending on the type of person you are. The neat-freak is going to spend more on doing laundry than the average student. Do you sneeze your way through the spring and fall? You might have to pay for allergy meds.

Top 10 Personal Expenses

1. **Laundry.** You need to do your laundry. You might be tempted to send out your laundry, but doing your own laundry saves a lot of money. Even so, factor in about $25 a month.

2. **Medical.** You'll be assessed a fee every time you visit the doctor or health clinic. If you take medication, prescriptions will also cost you a fair sum. Medical expenses are difficult to calculate—some students never get sick, while others are in and out of the doctor's office all winter long—so expect to spend anywhere from $50 to $500 a year.

3. **Clubs and organizations.** Planning on joining a fraternity/sorority or a campus club? Every group on campus will have dues and fees, ranging from $25 to $400.

4. **Food.** This is the one area where students often go over budget, so you might as well account for extra costs in your official budget. Even with a meal plan, if you buy one additional beverage a day, along with a bag of chips, a candy, or a protein bar, and split a pizza once a week, you've easily hit $50. There are also birthday dinner parties, roommate dinners, and food expenditures at movies, concerts, and sporting events. A conservative amount to budget would be $1,000.

Going Home

Booking way in advance makes traveling a lot cheaper, especially around holidays. Check your school's academic calendar to see which days you can travel on, and try to avoid traveling near the actual holidays.

5. **Travel.** Want to go camping for the weekend? You'll need some extra cash for that, and other, trips. Traveling home generally isn't an option—you'll need to do that. Fortunately, most students can get their folks to pay or at least pitch in. Depending on where you live, budget $250 to $1,000.

6. **Music.** You'll discover new music while at college, and you'll definitely want to buy CDs and go to concerts. Add another $300 to your budget. Borrow music from your friends whenever possible, and you'll easily knock this figure down.

7. **Duds.** At some point your hole-riddled wool sweater will become unwearable. You'll need new clothes now and again, so budget a modest $250.

8. **Hygiene.** Personal hygiene products can be pricey, especially if you're a fan of expensive shampoos and lotions. You *need* deodorant; you *want* $50 hair conditioner. You'll spend no less than $500 on these types of products.

9. **Transportation.** If you bring a car to campus, consider fuel, repairs, and insurance, which will run you as much as $2,000. If you don't have wheels, factor in public transportation costs. In a big city like New York, that can add up to $600 a year.

10. **Entertainment.** You'll want to keep an entertainment fund for movies, movie rentals, concerts, bowling, etc. There are many free events on campus; go to these as often as possible, and you'll hopefully keep your costs down to $500.

OK, so now you know how much cash you're going to need. But where is all that cash going to come from?

Student Loans

About a week to ten days after your college receives your loan funds (called *disbursement*) and subtracts what they need for tuition and fees, you should get a refund check—*but not in your first semester.* First-time loan borrowers of federal funds have to wait thirty days for the loan to be disbursed. So, it's a good idea to come to college with at least $400 in the bank (or more, if possible) while you're waiting for your loan to be processed.

Students usually spend more money at the beginning of the semester, so you'll want a cushion to make it through September.

Managing Your Loan

You should be able to check the status of your loan online, through the school's or lender's website. There, you will find when the money is going to be sent to the bursar's office, which collects charges and coordinates billing for all student expenses. At that point, your school should know how long it will take for you to get the difference. Mark the day on your calendar. Loans are given in two disbursements, at the beginning of each semester. So, just after you've gone broke over the holidays, you'll refill your account for the new year.

If your college has a direct-deposit option, sign up as soon as possible. Your money will arrive in your account much faster than if you sit around waiting for a check. Even so, make sure that the school always has your correct address. Some colleges allow students to pick up their loan checks from the bursar's office.

Scholarships and Grants

If you've earned a scholarship, the money is generally paid directly to the college, just like your loan money. The school deducts what it needs, then gives you the rest. If your scholarship requires you to meet certain requirements, such as keeping your grades up, then you'd better work hard. If your GPA slips because of difficulties at home, due to personal issues, or because you've gotten in over your head with difficult courses, see your advisor. There may be a way to hang on to that free money.

Student Health Insurance

Most college health insurance plans are a great bargain and offer superior and cheaper services than private plans. You can't get by in college without health insurance, and schools won't let you attend without it.

Grants

Grants, unlike scholarships, don't require that you maintain a certain GPA or meet other criteria, after you've received the cash. They are often *need-based*, or go to members of minority groups or alumni networks most in need of financial help. Again, these funds will be given to the college, then disbursed to you once your school has taken its share. Keep an eye on your student financial account to make sure that all grants coming to you have arrived and are being properly accounted for.

Your Bank Account

Start doing some research on the banks in the town. You'll find all the details you need on opening a new account on their websites. Some larger colleges offer their students accounts in their own credit union, generally where most of the school employees belong. In college towns, banks will offer special deals to students.

10 Things to Look for in a Bank Account

1. **Low costs.** Get the account with the lowest transaction fees. Banks charge for everything from cashing checks to ATM withdrawals. Also, look for a no-cost or low-cost account that won't hit you with big fees just for opening and maintaining an account; a few bucks a month adds up.

2. **No transaction limits.** Find an account that allows you to have plenty of free transactions per month. Figure out how many checks you'll write per month and how many times you'll access the ATM. Then add four transactions (one per week), just to be safe. If you can get this many transactions for free, you'll be fine.

3. **Low or no minimum balance.** Some banks offer great deals on accounts if you keep a certain balance,

but this amount will invariably be too high for you to maintain. Find a bank that allows you to have a low minimum balance without added fees. Student accounts often don't force you to maintain a certain balance.

4. **Overdraft protection.** An overdraft is the amount of money a bank will loan you when you cash a check, use a debit card, or have an automatic payment charged against an account that has too little money in it to cover the withdrawal. For example, if you have $150 in your account and you write a check for $175, you want a bank that won't *bounce* the check (have it returned with insufficient funds) but will instead lend you the $25 needed to let the check cash. Banks offer overdraft protection for a low annual fee, and some offer it for free if you carry a certain balance.

5. **Accessible ATMs.** Choose a bank that has a lot of ATM machines on or close to campus. Fees for taking money out of ATMs not affiliated with your bank can add up to a lot of money.

6. **Direct deposit.** Your account should have a direct deposit option so that your parents or employers can put money into your account without having to give you a check. Ideally, this option should be free.

7. **Debit card.** A debit card looks like a credit card and functions like one too, but the money comes directly out of your account, and you can use it at an ATM as well. Think of a debit card as a "check card": using one is like writing a virtual check.

8. **Online banking.** Choose a bank that allows you to manage your account and bills online. This will make life a lot easier.

9. **Interest.** If you can get an interest-bearing account that also meets all of the above requirements, more power to you. It's unlikely that you'll find one, and if you do, the interest will be low. Don't let interest be a big deciding factor.

10. **Gifts.** OK, gifts are the last thing you should consider, but, all things being equal, go with the bank that gives you a gift for opening your account. Cell phones, money vouchers, and other gifts are tempting. Just don't let these gifts sway you into opening a bank account that doesn't suit your needs.

Balancing Your Checkbook

Balancing your checkbook means keeping track of your account by sub-tracting withdrawals and adding deposits. Doing this simple task helps you find bank errors (it does happen) and helps you keep track of how much cash you have in your account.

You can balance as you go along, or you can do it at the end of the month when your monthly bank statement arrives. Back in the Stone Age, every-one did their balancing with an old-fashioned pencil and the register in their checkbook. Today, there is cheap and easy-to-use software that will even download your bank statements right into your computer and auto-balance your account. It doesn't get easier than that. But if you want to do it using brainpower, remember these 10 steps:

1. Read your bank statement carefully to make sure that all the withdrawals and deposits are yours.

2. Be sure to check for extra fees—you'll see how most of these are avoidable.

3. Keep all receipts or print-outs of online transactions, and write down anything else that doesn't come with a receipt.

4. Remember, the current balance on your ATM receipt isn't always up-to-date.

5. Keep track of all checks you've written. Has every check you've written for the month cleared? Your balance may be lower once these checks clear.

123	9/20	COLLEGE BOOKSTORE			$831.75
deposit	9/22	BIRTHDAY CHECK/GRANDMA	$100.00		
withdraw	9/27	ATM			$40.00

6. Don't forget to keep track of bank fees.

7. Remember to add interest earned, if any.

8. Only write checks against money you know you have in your account. Checks used to take more than a week to clear, but that time has been cut down significantly.

9. If your calculations are a little bit off, try to remember what you've missed. ATM fees? Those shoes you bought with your debit card?

10. If your balance is still off, go back and make sure that you wrote things down correctly. It's easy to transpose numbers.

Bills

If you live on campus, you're not going to have any utility bills, though you will be charged for long-distance phone calls. If you have a cell phone, you'll have to deal with that bill as well, unless your parents have offered to pay it for the time being.

If you're living off campus you will have many bills: rent, electricity, phone, water, and gas, to name a few. If you have roommates, don't put all the bills under one name. If they're all in your name, you may have to go hounding your roommates for the money, and you'll have to pay the bill anyway, even if they don't have the cash. If you don't pay, you can ruin your credit, even if it's not your fault that your roommates are bums. Share the burden.

Emergency Funds

The financial aid office or student affairs office will often loan you some cash in an emergency. These loans are generally short-term, small ($200–$500), and interest free. These funds generally need to be paid back by the end of the semester.

Save Something

Maybe you have a nice little allowance and your part-time job is paying enough to pad your bank account. Great! Now try to save some of that cash. There will be something you'll need or want in the future, and you'll be glad to have some cash stashed away. Emergencies crop up as well, and it's nice to be financially flexible at those times. The best way to save is to not spend in the first place. There are no real tricks to saving: just refrain from buying things and wasting money.

Long-Term Savings

You'll want to have some money set aside for when you graduate, and it's never too early to start saving for that moment, especially if you're going to be paying off loans.

10
WAYS
To Save

1. **Coffee.** There are not many things cheaper than a cup of coffee . . . unless, of course, you buy it at one of those pricey coffee joints where you have to take out a loan just to get a cappuccino. Invest in a coffee maker and brew it yourself for pennies a day.

2. **Phone calls.** Find out when you can call at the lowest long-distance rate. Many cell phone plans give you free calling in the evenings and on weekends. There's no need to rack up a phone bill when you can talk for free.

3. **Campus events.** A lot of events on campus will include a box lunch, snacks, beverages, and other free stuff.

4. **Movies.** Buy bottled beverages and snacks outside of the movie theater and bring them in.

5. **Sales.** If you really want a luxury item, wait for it to go on sale or do some comparison shopping and find it online.

6. **Used books.** Always try to buy used books. If you can't find them in your town, look online.

7. **Smoking.** If you smoke, do whatever you have to do to stop. Cigarettes are expensive, and they're not getting any cheaper.

8. **Food.** Eat at all-you-can-eat buffets when you go out. They're generally cheap and offer something for everyone. But don't say we didn't warn you about the "freshman fifteen" a few chapters back.

9. **Garage sales.** Hunt for garage sales on the weekend if there's something you need. Don't just go to browse or you'll end up buying junk you don't need.

10. **Used clothing.** Aside from looking stylish, you'll save tons of money if you buy your clothes secondhand. Learn to ask, "Can you do better on the price?" They almost always can.

There's a grace period of six months after you leave college before you have to start paying back your loans, but interest will still capitalize, which means that the loan amount will grow if you don't pay the interest as it accrues. Not paying back your loans is called *defaulting,* which will destroy your credit and make it nearly impossible to get another government loan, not to mention a loan to buy a home or a car. And forget about ever getting a credit card.

Credit Cards

When you use a credit card, a company (usually a bank) is giving you a loan based on your promise to repay the money. For this convenient service, they charge you interest on all of your purchases—this is how they make money. Each month, you have to pay a minimum balance on your credit card. The longer you take to pay back the remaining balance, the more interest you accrue. When you don't pay back what you've spent, you lose your credit standing, and it takes a long time to get back.

You'll find booths all over campus trying to get you to apply for credit cards. They'll even give you a free T-shirt or Frisbee if you fill out the form. Only apply for credit cards if you really think you can be responsible with them. They're not free money! You have to pay back every cent you charge, including interest. Yes, they are convenient, but they're not to be confused with actual money.

Building Credit

Taking out student loans in your name and having a credit card are a great way to build credit, as long as you don't default on them. Using a credit card every once in a while and then paying off the balance each month shows future creditors that you're a good credit risk. Having good credit is crucial and affords you a measure of fiscal security that you're going to appreciate later when you want to buy a car or a home.

"By the time I graduated college I had managed to accrue over $6,000 in debt on my credit cards. If I had it to do over again, I wouldn't have even applied for one."

Lesley H.
Brown University

10

PART-TIME JOBS
For College Students

1
Babysitter

2
Tutor

3
Dog walker/sitter

4
Grocery bagger

5
Burger flipper

6
Coffee slinger

7
Paper filer

8
Data-entry clerk

9
Movie ticket taker

10
Server/barista

Part-Time Jobs

Unless your parents are sending you a hefty allowance, you're going to need some pocket cash. Getting a part-time job is the way to go. Part-time jobs for college students aren't all that difficult to find. They don't pay a ton, but they're better than being broke, and if you can find work in a food joint, then some of your meals will be covered too. You'll be able to find a job even if you don't have any job experience. Ideally, you'll only work fifteen to twenty hours a week. Any more than that and you risk sacrificing your GPA.

"I worked in a preschool as an assistant during my first year of college. The hours were flexible and it paid OK. The only real problem with that job was that I caught every cold and stomach bug that those kids got!"

Priscilla Y.
American University

The Job Search

Your first stop should be your school's career center. They often have job listings that are perfect for college students. Local parents (sometimes professors at the university) put ads into the career center's database looking for babysitters and tutors. Many career centers have job fairs throughout the year that are a great resource for part-time jobs and internships. Try to make a good impression on the people behind the booths at the job fairs: they just might be the people interviewing you some day.

Next, check the classified ads in your local newspaper. If there's a particular place you think you'd enjoy working, walk in and ask to speak with the manager to find out they're hiring. Always ask to fill out an application.

Be prepared to fill out a ton of paperwork. There are a lot of other people who want the same job, but if you keep at it you'll eventually land a job you'll be happy with. Apply at places where you think your odds are slim: other people have the same doubts, so there are likely to be fewer applicants. Hey, you never know.

Federal Work-Study

Financial aid packages often include money through the Federal Work-Study program. The federal government gives schools money that they can use to employ students on campus. Colleges love this program, because it's free labor for them. The jobs tend to be menial and often pay minimum wage. There are some good ones to be had, however, and unlike part-time jobs, your pay from work-study jobs is not reported as income, so it's not taxable. Plus, your employer tends to be more flexible than a regular employer and you get to work with other students, faculty, and staff on campus. Those connections can lead to bigger, better things.

Campus Jobs

Working on campus is convenient, though it doesn't pay much and the work is often menial. At certain times of the year, like during registration, your school may need extra hands and will hire students on a temporary basis. Schools often need students to work at events on campus. These jobs aren't always advertised, so ask your RA, your professors, or other campus employees if they know of any job opportunities.

Internships

An internship is a low-paying job that offers you college credit in exchange for "real world" experience. Generally, the internship you want will be in a field that you're interested in pursuing. Because you're a first-year student and you might not be sure what your major will be, you have the benefit of choosing something that simply sounds interesting. First years may not be offered internships during the regular academic year, but summer internships after your first year are common.

Since we're talking about money here, we have to mention that some internships don't pay a thing. Nada. Zilch. But you might get college credit. So, check your bank account and ask yourself whether you would benefit most from a part-time job or an unpaid internship.

The Interview

There's an art to performing well on an interview. Counselors at the career center will coach you and help you hone your interview skills. Don't go on any interviews until you've practiced, because other people who are less qualified than you will have come prepared.

10 Job Interview Tips

1. **Bring a résumé and cover letter.** The folks at the career center can help you with both. Even if you're applying to The Coffee Nook, you'll want a professional résumé and cover letter. These things will make you stand out from the other potential coffee slingers.

2. **Dress appropriately.** If the employees at The Coffee Nook are wearing jeans and T-shirts, you wear jeans and your nicest T-shirt to the interview, not a suit. If you're interviewing for an office job, dress up.

3. **Don't chew gum.** Shouldn't this be obvious?

4. **Make eye contact.** Eye contact shows confidence. Don't stare, however. You don't want to creep out the interviewer. While you're add it, smile!

5. **Be positive.** Try to turn every negative into a positive. If the interviewer asks you to name three of your biggest weaknesses, you can say, "Well, I tend to be a perfectionist. I often work too hard. I also tend to work so quickly that I'll often ask for more tasks."

Guinea Pigs for Hire

If you're at a large research university with lots of graduate students, consider being a guinea pig for some of their experiments. Labs will pay well over minimum wage to conduct research on you. The psychology department is a great place to start.

6. **Spin, spin, spin.** You might not have a lot of experience in the job market, but surely you've done *something* for cash. For example, if you've helped a neighbor pick rocks out of her garden, you can call that "landscaping."

7. **Ask questions.** Ask at least three pertinent questions about the job. For example, ask what your duties will be, how you can best be of service in the job, and what they're looking for in an employee. Do *not* ask self-serving questions too early in the interview. Toward the end, you can ask how much the job pays and what the hours are.

8. **Use buzz words.** Do a little research about the job and the company and use the jargon associated with both.

9. **Be honest.** The worst thing you can do in an interview is lie. You can embellish a little, but that's about it. If you lie about having a lot of experience doing something, you'll most certainly get caught later when you screw things up.

10. **Get recommendations.** Try to get good recommendations from people who know you to be a good worker or at least a good person. This way you can name those people on your job application with confidence that they'll say nice things about you.

Keeping a Job

Once you've gotten the job, be prepared to be productive and positive. Yes, we know you'd probably rather be anywhere else than working behind a counter in that lovely smock, but you're there for a reason. Try to have fun with it. Some jobs are a blast, while others are a drag. The good news is that you won't be doing it forever. And that paycheck is awfully nice.

If you absolutely hate the job, try to stay there for at least a whole semester. Then, when you give notice, you

Taxes

If you work, you're going to pay taxes. You don't have to worry too much about this, because your employer will be taking money out of your paycheck automatically. You have until April 15 each year to file last year's tax return.

can say that your new course load is going to be so tough that you need the extra time to study. That way you can leave on good terms and potentially get a recommendation from that employer. Also, the longer you stay in a job while you're in college, the better it looks on your résumé. Always give your employer two weeks' notice.

The only time you can ditch a job abruptly is if you get an opportunity that you just can't pass up and that will add value to your education and your life. Ditching Burger Heaven for a paid internship at Microsoft is going to be worthwhile.

The Bottom Line

The bottom line on cash is this: it's not easy to come by, but it's easy to spend. Careful budgeting, getting a job, and working to build good credit will give you real world experience that you'll need when you graduate. Monitor every penny that comes in and out of your bank account so that you get a handle on your earning and spending. It sounds difficult, but what's truly difficult is walking around broke all the time because you didn't bother to budget.

STUDYING

"College is like a fountain of knowledge—and students are there to drink."

Anonymous

Good study skills are the key to success in college. We know you studied a lot in high school; after all, you wouldn't have gotten into college without having some study skills. But you have to take studying to the next level once you arrive at college.

Study Habits

A habit is a pattern of behavior defined by frequent repetition. Many college students don't ever really catch the habit of studying and end up doing it on the fly, as time allows. We suggest you make studying a habitual part of your week, something that becomes part of your routine, so much so that you do it without thinking. (Clarification: we want you to think *while* studying, just not when you sit down to start.)

Memorization

Studying is often about recalling information for the short term, like memorizing dates for a history test, which you then promptly forget. Improving your memory is tough: some of us are just more absent-minded than others. But what you *can* do is improve your memory habits—that is, *how* you remember things.

You should employ all of your senses when trying to memorize facts. Here's how you do it:

Sight. Write down everything you have to remember and then look at it over and over again, visualizing what it means. The act of writing adds "muscle memory" to the memorization process.

Sound. Say everything you need to remember aloud. Tape yourself reading the facts and play the tape continually before the test.

Scent, Touch, and Taste. These three senses are a bit trickier. The simplest way to exploit them is to attach a smell, a texture, or a flavor to something you need to remember. For example, smell an onion and then recite a fact you need to know that begins with the letter *O*, then do the same with a lemon for something that begins with the letter *L*, and so on. While taking the test, recall the smell, texture, or flavor and the fact attached to it will come back to you.

You may find it difficult to associate everything you're trying to memorize to one of your five senses, so try to assign the facts that are giving you the most trouble to each sense. If there's a math formula you keep forgetting, create a sensory clue that helps you remember it.

Concentration

Concentration is essential to learning. If your brain is running like a hamster on a wheel, facts won't sink in. With that mind, here are 10 tips for maintaining your concentration while studying:

1. Put what you've just studied into your own words, as if you're going to teach it to another student.

2. Write down what you don't understand then find the answers in the text or your notes.

3. Visualize yourself studying. Imagine that you can see yourself from the outside. Do you look like someone who's concentrating? Or are you tapping your pencil and daydreaming?

4. Try not to eat while you study. Save that for study breaks.

5. Study in a quiet space. If people are talking around you, or if music is playing, you may find yourself tuning in to those sounds and tuning out your work.

6. Study alone. Having a friend by your side when you study can be a real distraction. If your physics textbook is boring you to tears, you can bet the farm you'll suddenly remember some crucial piece of gossip you need to share with your best buddy at that very moment.

7. Don't study right before you have a meeting or appointment. You'll be stressed about the next thing you have to do, and you won't be able to focus on the task at hand.

10
Memorization Tips

1   **Pay attention.** This may seem obvious, but it's important. If you're drifting and daydreaming, you won't remember a thing.

2   **Plan to recall.** If you actively know that you have to remember something, you are more likely to remember it.

3   **Review facts just after class.** If you spend fifteen minutes just after class reviewing your notes, you are far more likely to retain the information.

4   **Study a lot.** This also seems like common sense, but the more you go over the material, the more you will retain it.

5   **Link a new fact to an old one.** Let's say you've just been told in class that lemons grow on trees. You already know that apples grow on trees. Link lemons to apples and you'll remember where lemons grow.

6   **Don't cram.** You'll remember more if you study the material in short bursts rather than during marathon all-nighters.

7   **Use shapes.** Visualize the fact inside a shape, then write it inside the shape and cut the shape out so you can feel its curves and edges. You can even color the shape if that helps, or make the shape out of something textured, like vinyl or sandpaper. Draw the shape on a piece of scrap paper during the test, and the fact should come back to you.

8   **Create diagrams and webs.** Linking facts together with diagrams and webs can help you remember details. For example, write the names of different Civil War generals in boxes and draw lines connecting them to the battles they fought in. That way you'll also memorize where they overlap.

9   **Link numbers to one another.** If you need to remember new numbers, think of how they relate to numbers you already have memorized. Let's say you need to remember that the Civil War began in 1861. Let's also say your dorm room phone number ends with 61. Is your relationship with your roommate civil? Either way, you've linked roommates to civil. Now all you have to do is remember the 18 and you're one answer closer to an A.

10 **Learn to rap.** Well, not really—learn to rhyme. Find a rhyme for a key word or fact. To use an example you're probably familiar with, rhyming "1492" with "ocean blue" helps you remember when Columbus first came to the Americas. Also check out **www. sparknotes.com/newsat/flocabulary** where you'll find our "flocabulary raps"!

8. Give yourself an anti-daydreaming mantra. When you find yourself drifting off, you can say, "Come back, [your name]," or some other short phrase.

9. Think about what's motivating you to study. Are you trying to pass a test, pass the class, get extra credit, impress your parents, keep your status on the dean's list, or meet a personal goal? Keeping your eye on the prize should bring back your focus.

10. Set reasonable goals for yourself. If you're unrealistic about how long you're going to study or what you're going to accomplish, your concentration will fade as you become increasingly frustrated.

Keep in mind that all these tips won't work for everyone. Some people need to listen to music or have a study buddy to keep them focused. Try all these methods and determine which ones work best for you.

Time Management

College is a time-drainer. Well, more accurately, college life is a time-drainer. College classes themselves take up only about twelve to fifteen hours of your week, far less than a part-time job, or even high school classes for that matter. But it's all the other stuff you have to negotiate—parties, friends, studying, eating, doing laundry—that can be a real time suck. Learning to manage your time will help you get through college, as well as life, successfully. It's an invaluable life skill, and you need to start working on it now.

TIPS
For Time Management

1. **Do the tough stuff first.** Work on the material you really hate, or that you're not great at, before doing other stuff. That way you'll have energy when you need it the most.

2. **Remember the 3-1 rule.** Plan to study three hours for every class credit. For example, if your English class earns you three credits, you should spend nine hours studying for it each week.

3. **Avoid all-nighters.** Pulling an all-nighter before a test, or cramming in general, is not only a poor way to learn but also leaves you sleepy on test day. You're better off studying all week and then getting a good night's sleep the night before.

4. **Study on your time.** When are you fresh and most alert? If you are focused first thing in the morning, set that time aside for studying. If you work really well at 3 A.M., schedule your study time for then.

5. **Work while you wait.** Use your time sitting in the health center waiting room or in the laundry room to study.

6. **Set a study goal.** Always ask yourself, "What do I need to accomplish in this study session?"

7. **Set time limits.** Set aside time to study and *stop when the time is up*. This should help you focus while you're studying, because you know when it'll come to an end.

8. **Take five.** Well, fifteen, actually. Allow yourself a fifteen-minute break for each hour of studying. Get up, stretch, have a snack—then get back to the books.

9. **Get in the right frame of mind.** Get into the right frame of mind before you begin studying. If you have something else on your mind, you'll find yourself easily distracted by it.

10. **Try to stick to a schedule.** We say *try* because it's tough to keep a set schedule in college. Everyone seems to want a slice of your time. Do the best you can to schedule everything from studying to doing laundry.

Prioritizing

A priority is something that's more important than something else, such as studying for a test instead of going to a party. Make a personal priority list, including the 10 most important things you need to do each week. And, by all means, be honest about it! Do you really feel that going to class is a priority? Do you really place studying over partying and hanging out with friends in the dorm? Here's a sample list:

1. Studying
2. Partying
3. Going to class
4. Playing sports
5. Hanging out with friends
6. Watching movies
7. Reading
8. Eating
9. Spending time with boyfriend/girlfriend
10. Sleeping

With a pair of scissors, cut out each of the 10 things. Next, ask your friends, a professor, your RA, and your advisor to place the activities in order of importance. Write down their responses and compare them to your original list. Are their lists a reality check, or were you on track from the start?

Your Date Book (or PDA)

Your best friend in college isn't going to be your roommate, but your date book or PDA. Without it, we can guarantee you won't be able to keep track of everything you need to do.

TIPS

For Creating Your Schedule

1 Write down when you have to be in class.

2 Give yourself between fifteen minutes and half an hour before each class to review your notes.

3 Write down everywhere else you have to be: job, club meetings, sports practice, and so on.

4 Write down three mealtimes a day.

5 Schedule study times—remember, three hours for each class credit.

6 Block out some time each day for your personal needs, like doing laundry or buying dorm room provisions.

7 Schedule leisure time on two weekdays. Thursday night is usually "college night"—time to party and go out—so that might be a good time to set aside for fun.

8 Block out most of the weekend for fun stuff. You'll have to use Sunday for some studying, but if you work hard during the week, you won't have to spend Friday and Saturday night in the library playing catch-up.

9 Schedule things that don't necessarily happen every week, like roommate meetings and dorm meetings.

10 Schedule at least nine hours for sleep (that includes the time it takes you to fall asleep at night and get out of bed in the morning).

Sample Schedule

MONDAY	
8:00–8:30 A.M.	Wake up and shower
8:30–9:00 A.M.	Eat breakfast
9:00–10:00 A.M.	Bio 101
10:00 A.M.–12:00 P.M.	Study for history exam
12:00–1:00 P.M.	Lunch
1:00–2:00 P.M.	Chem Lab
2:00–3:00 P.M.	Work out at gym
3:00–4:30 P.M.	English seminar
4:30–6:00 P.M.	Do laundry/study
6:00–7:00 P.M.	Dinner
7:00–8:00 P.M.	Model UN meeting
8:00–10:00 P.M.	Study for bio midterm
10:00 P.M.–12:00 A.M.	Movie with roommates
12:00 A.M.	Sleep

Where to Study

Once you've perfected your study habits, you have to find the right place to apply them. Some people are better off studying in absolute peace and quiet, while others are happy to play music or sit in a busy coffee shop. Try both and stick with whichever one works best for you.

10 Study Space Tips

1. Try not to study in your room all the time. There are too many distractions there, like the television, the phone, and your roommates.
2. Have a regular study area, a place that's yours, like a cubicle in the library or your favorite chair in a coffee shop.
3. Find a place where you feel safe and undisturbed.
4. Find a place where you can sit forever without being kicked out.

5. Whatever you do, don't study in bed. Your body is used to sleeping in bed, and you're likely to fall asleep if you study there. Which is more appealing: taking a nap or finishing that economics paper? Exactly.

6. Choose a quiet place. The dorm is noisy, so the library is a better choice for those who can't tune out noise.

7. Avoid places with visual distractions. Lots of commotion can be more distracting than lots of noise.

8. Don't get too comfortable. Your focus will fade if you're too cozy.

9. Don't let others disturb you. If you do study in your dorm room, hang a "Do Not Disturb" sign on your door. Hopefully your dormmates will respect it.

10. If you lose concentration in one study space, find another one rather than trying to make the original spot work.

Shorthand

Writing notes in shorthand will save you precious time. Here are some common abbreviations:

+	plus/and
=	equals/means the same thing as
@	at
>	more important
<	less important
e.g.	for example
i.e.	that is
cf.	compare
et al.	and others
ex.	example

Taking Notes

While most of what you hear in lecture will be on the test, much of it may not be in your textbook. The professor will hit the main points during the lecture, so be sure to attend all of them, even if attendance isn't taken. Make sure you have the right tools for note-taking: a good pen or pencil and a three-punch notebook so you can add pages between your notes. If you miss something the professor says, don't panic: you can get it later from a friend in class. It's better to continue taking notes than to frantically go back, which will cause you to miss more of the lecture. Finally, pay attention and be alert. A daydreamer doesn't take great notes.

10 Note-Taking Tips

1. Sit as close as possible to the professor so you can hear everything.

2. Write legibly enough for you to decipher your own handwriting.

3. Use a computer or PDA in class if you type faster than you write by hand.

4. Tape-record lectures if your professors allow it. This isn't a replacement for taking notes, however, because you could easily have a technical issue with the recorder and miss the entire lecture. To be on the safe side, do both.

5. Put asterisks near important concepts and arrows near concepts you don't really understand.

6. Copy everything the professor writes on the board or the overhead projector.

7. As you take notes, summarize things in your own words instead of trying to write everything verbatim.

8. Identify the main points of the lecture, which are generally introduced when the professor lists concepts, changes topic, or repeats information.

9. Use your own method of shorthand, making sure you're consistent and you understand what these symbols and abbreviations mean when you review your notes.

10. After class, take a few minutes to review, organize, and expand your notes. You will only remember this information for about an hour, so make sure to take some time for this important step.

Note-Taking Services

You'll often find note-taking services online or near campus. These companies are run by entrepreneurs who make a buck by selling notes from large lectures and core classes, often classes held by the professors you'll have in your first year. You can usually buy a whole semester's worth of notes. These days, students are also likely to post their notes online as well.

Is this cheating? Well, not unless you use the notes instead of going to class. You also don't really know if the notes are good or not. What if the person taking the notes missed an important point in the lecture and you miss that question on the test? It's not worth the risk. While store-bought-notes can be a good study aid, they're not a replacement for going to class and taking your own notes.

Be careful about selling your notes to a company that publishes them. A lot of colleges are cracking down on these companies, claiming that they are stealing the schools' intellectual property. The final word isn't out yet on whether a lecture given orally can be copyrighted (right now, they can't). However, once the professor types up and distributes lecture notes, it is copyrightable and can't be legally sold or posted online by students or note-taking companies.

Margin Notes

Making margin notes in your textbooks is essential to remembering and processing what you've read. If you plan on writing a lot, you should write in pencil and erase everything at the end of the semester, which will allow you to resell your books.

10 Tips for Taking Margin Notes

1. Read a chapter or section thoroughly before making any notes. Write notes during your second read-through.
2. Underline important points and main ideas.
3. Circle important dates.
4. Bracket important names.
5. Use shorthand marks consistently.
6. Briefly summarize each page at the top.
7. Write the definitions of unfamiliar words at the bottom of the page where they appear.
8. Use the front and back covers for keeping your own index of important points in the book, as well as your own glossary of key terms.
9. Use a highlighter to mark important points. It can't be erased, but, as far as we're concerned, a good grade is more important than possibly not being able to sell back your book. Highlight away!

Borrowing Notes

If you miss a lecture, borrow notes from a classmate, but be sure to choose a classmate who's getting good grades. Pay to have the notes photocopied. Students don't really want to let go of the only copy of their notes, so don't expect someone to tear them out of a notebook and hand them to you.

10. After you're done taking margin notes, write your understanding of the chapter or section in your own words on a sheet of paper. Fold and place the sheet of paper at the beginning of the chapter.

Study Groups

Forming a study group of three to six people is a great way to share information, get answers, fill in the holes in your notes, and make studying fun. Find a few people in your class who are interested in getting together to study. You can meet in someone's dorm room, the talking section of the library, the dining hall, a coffee shop, or a meeting room requested from the university.

One person should be the group leader, organizing the "where," "when," and "who" of the group. The leader also organizes the agenda for each meeting, outlining what the group is going to talk about and in what order. Each person is responsible for bringing some study material. For example, if you're studying a novel, someone will bring research on the characters and someone else will bring research on the significance of the setting.

Study groups require a bit of trial and error. You'll have to meet a few times to really get into the groove of your particular dynamic. Once the hour or two of studying is over, go out for pizza together and discuss how you think the group worked and what could be done better the next time.

Preparing for Exams

Start studying hard for an exam one week before you take it. Study alone, with a friend, and with a study group, devoting at least an hour each day to the topic. Go over your class notes and outline the important points on a separate sheet of paper. Then highlight the material

Skimming

Skimming means glancing over a piece of writing quickly, looking for key terms and the main idea. You can skim a text after you've read it once, but don't use skimming as a first read. If you do, you're guaranteed to miss something important.

you're sure you know backward and forward. Once you've done that, you'll know what you need to focus on.

On another sheet of paper, list the unhighlighted material. Clarify each point using the textbook, a friend, the internet, or your professor. Next, make flashcards for any material you're unsure about, and have someone quiz you until you know the material cold.

Flashcards

Flashcards are a great way to study for an exam. You probably made flashcards in high school to memorize SAT vocabulary or to remember a mind-numbingly long list of dates for a history exam.

There are many benefits to creating and using flashcards. First, they can be shuffled, which means you won't just be memorizing the order in which facts appear in a textbook or lecture. If your professors are even half as smart as you think they are, they won't repeat facts this way. Second, the act of creating flashcards helps you remember facts. The simple act of writing a date, formula, or definition uses a different part of your brain than when you read. Third, you can always add more flashcards to your pile. Forgot the year in which the Constitutional Convention convened? No problem: just create a new flashcard and shuffle it into your stack.

Procrastination

Some students procrastinate because studying is boring or difficult. Others procrastinate because they'd rather go out and have fun than study. Whatever the reason for procrastinating, the result is the same: cramming, crunching, stressing, and setbacks. Everyone procrastinates, but you can learn to do it less often.

How do you know when you're procrastinating? When you find yourself saying, "I'll study after *The Real World* is over," or "I'll write that paper after I clean my entire room, my suitemate's room, the communal bathroom, and the hall," then you know you're procrastinating. Here are some ways to get around it:

Make a to-do list for the next day before you go to bed at night. Make sure that you actually have time to do all the things on your list. Then do everything on the list, crossing things off as you go. Put some really easy tasks on the list so you get a sense of accomplishment when you cross them off. Brushing your teeth and going to class? Done and done.

Break complicated tasks down into smaller chunks. For example, if you have to write a paper, instead of adding "write paper" to your schedule, write:

1. outline paper
2. research topic
3. summarize paper
4. define thesis
5. write first paragraph
6. write rest of paper
7. do footnotes (or endnotes)
8. EDIT
9. proofread
10. have someone else proofread

10 More Study Tips

1. Let go of the perfectionist within. Believing that you have to do everything perfectly is a recipe for not getting anything done. You don't have to be perfect, and knowing that can be liberating.

2. Set aside specific times to study. When the time is up, stop studying.

3. Schedule study time with someone else. That way you're accountable for showing up and getting your work done.

4. Get—and stay—organized. Studying is less daunting if you know exactly what you have to do.

5. Be aware of how you procrastinate so you can call yourself on it when it happens.

LAST-MINUTE
Exam Tips

We're not advocating cramming for tests: these are last-minute ways to reinforce the intense studying you've done all week and to ensure success when taking a test.

1   If you've made flashcards (and we recommend you do), flip through them just before the exam.

2   Repeat vocabulary words, facts, and formulas to yourself.

3   Skim the text.

4   Read over your notes.

5   Discuss the material with someone else in the class an hour before the exam.

6   When you get the exam, read the directions carefully.

7   Immediately write all formulas you've memorized on the top of the test.

8   Answer the easiest questions first.

9   For essay questions, make sure you're answering the exact question, not writing around the topic in the hopes that your professor won't notice you have no idea what you're taking about.

10 Write legibly: neatness always counts.

6. Think about how procrastination makes you feel. Most people feel stressed while they're procrastinating. Think about how good you'll feel when you finish all your studying.

7. Try making a task more fun. Play your favorite music while doing it or include a friend/study partner.

8. Reward yourself. When you're done with the task, do something fun or eat something yummy.

9. Weigh your success. How will succeeding in the task at hand change the rest of your day? How will it change your week?

10. Remember that there's not enough time in the day to get everything done. Just do what you can today.

Asking for an Extension

If you're really strapped for time and you haven't studied enough (or at all), or if something has come up and you haven't even started your paper by the due date, you can ask for an extension. Try not to lie. Just tell your professor you need some more time. Most profs are pretty good about helping you out if you have a valid excuse. If your grandmother dies four times during the semester and you have your appendix out twice—well, you may be out of luck.

IDENTITY

"Your identity is what you have committed yourself to. You build meaning into your life through your commitments—whether to your religion, to your conception of an ethical order, to your family, group, or community, to the rights of others, to unborn generations."

John W. Gardner

Your College Identity

High school students are often pegged by their classmates as single-minded characters: you've got your jocks, your geeks, your freaks, your nice girls, your bullies, your cheerleaders, your Prom Kings and Queens, your honor students, and your stoners. Once you are typecast into one of these roles, it's pretty hard to shake off the label. Sadly, high school doesn't reward individuality.

But the moment you arrive at college, you shed these labels and become a blank slate. No one's going to remember that you snorted milk out of your nose all over the lunch table in ninth grade. And no one's going to know how envious everybody was when the popular boy asked you to the prom.

In college, you'll meet a whole new set of people who expect you to be a complex person with quirks and depth, a person who plays by his or her own rules. The first year of college is your big chance to focus on those personal qualities you've always wanted to refine or to give yourself a whole new identity. You're also going to experience a lot of personal freedom: you'll get to wear what you want and you'll even get to argue with your teachers without fear of punishment. In fact, debate is encouraged. The question is: how are you going to handle this new personal freedom?

In this chapter, we'll give you some advice about how to break out of that high school mold and become the person you *really* want to be. Most first-year students are looking for that big change in their lives, so get ready to embrace it!

Challenge Your Thinking

We are not necessarily saying that you're going to become a whole new person or that you're going to abandon everything you've ever believed in. If you have strong convictions when you enter college, critical thinking won't require you to change your mind. Being critical of what you see and hear means pondering ideas in new ways and allowing that experience to enrich the way you already think. As your knowledge and experience of the outer world expands, your inner world expands too.

Debate

Don't force yourself to become a blank slate: by all means, feel free to hang on to your old ideas. Some of them won't change at all, and that's OK. Perhaps you'll have an influence on other people and be the one to challenge *their* thinking.

But the one thing you do have to do is listen. Once you feel that you understand a new idea, then you can begin to challenge it and enter into debate. A good debate over hot issues is healthy and promotes learning. Just don't take it too much to heart. Allow other people to have their own opinions and try not to judge others for having a opinion different from your own.

You Will Change By . . .

- **Busting stereotypes.** You'll meet new people who, until now, you may have only stereotyped. If you give everyone a chance to become a real person, not just a part of a group that you have preconceived notions about, you'll definitely learn something valuable.

- **Experiencing culture.** If you're going to a university in a large urban setting, you'll have access to museums, theaters, and libraries. But even the smallest college town will have a unique history and interesting cultural opportunities.

- **Becoming a "townie."** OK, you're not going to become a real townie, but living in the town for four years means you'll become part of the community. Integrating into any community that's different from your hometown changes how you think, feel, and live.

- **Doing research.** Learning how to do academic research will transform the way you approach your schoolwork.

What Do You Think?

Challenging your thinking is what college is all about. No matter where you're enrolled or what you major in, college will challenge your worldview and personal values on every level, thus transforming your identity.

- **Modifying your environment.** Get ready for a change of space. If you're used to the salt flats of Utah, you might feel a little cramped sharing a little room with a roommate in Chicago. If you're used to urban life, imagine what the open space of the countryside will do to your personality.
- **Finding new foods.** What you eat changes who you are. If you go to a "crunchy granola" college in the West, perhaps you'll be inspired to become a vegetarian. If you go to school in Texas, maybe meat will become a staple in your diet.
- **Discovering new hobbies.** Your college town might provide you with all sorts of hobbies you never dreamed possible. If you're going to school on one of the coasts, you might take up windsurfing. If you're along the Appalachian Trail, you might discover hiking.
- **Getting around in new ways.** How you move from place to place in your new town will shift your perceptions. Are you a driver who is about to be thrust into a subway world? Or are you an urban diehard who never dreamed she would ever *really* get to drive a car around a hot desert town?
- **Moving at a new pace.** Without a doubt, the pace of life in Manhattan is faster than in Austin, Texas. Once you get used to a new pace it becomes part of your identity, and it's a tough thing to shake. If you're from a small town, you may have gotten used to saying "good morning" to everyone you pass on the street. That's going to be pretty much impossible in a large urban setting. If you're from a big city, you'll have to learn how to chat about the weather with the grocery clerk before he or she rings up your items.
- **Digging diversity.** In college, you will be exposed to different people with different views. Listening to new opinions is an enriching and valuable experience that will change you forever.

Your Personal Identity

Beyond learning about Asian art, organic chemistry, and women's history in college, you will learn a lot about the world through the people you meet. You'll have new friends, roommates, classmates, and professors who come from different socioeconomic groups, religions, ethnicities, and sexual orientations. In discovering your differences and commonalities with others, you'll sharpen your own identity.

Ethnicity

Your ethnicity includes your heritage, culture, history, and rituals. Many applications and forms have little boxes that ask you to identify your ethnicity: which box do you check? Do you leave this section blank? On a very basic level, that's how you identify yourself.

If you want to learn more about your own ethnic background, or if you just want to bond with other students from a background that's similar to yours, check out some of the student associations on campus. On most campuses you'll find Asian/Pacific Islander, Latino/Latina, African-American, and Native American student associations, among many others.

Religion

If you have strong religious convictions, there's no reason why you can't continue to practice religion in college. Nearly all colleges have resources that direct students to their local church, synagogue, mosque, or temple, and many schools have these institutions right on campus. The office of student life will be able to direct you to student clubs and associations, such as the Jewish Student Association (often called Hillel), the Catholic Student Association, and the Islamic Student Association.

Maybe you were never religious to begin with, but you've decided that now is the time to explore spirituality. Religious or meditative disciplines may give you the strength to develop your personal identity. If you're interested in learning about a religion, attend some on-campus religious services: you will certainly be welcome. Many campuses also have opportunities to get involved

Losing Your Religion?

Keep your feet on the ground and remember that you have a right to hold fast to the identity you've already shaped within your family. But also remember that as an adult, you have the right to change your beliefs.

in Buddhist meditation, drum circles, and martial arts. If your school doesn't seem to offer anything that interests you, keep an eye out for flyers that announce Bible studies, group meditation, and yoga. Remember, you can be spiritual without being religious.

Gender

College is a time to question gender roles and to determine if you're comfortable with the role you've been assigned. If you're interested in exploring why men and women behave the way they do and want to know how to break out of these cultural roles, take a Gender Studies course. These may be science courses that examine how researchers have studied men's and women's bodies, or they may be humanities courses that look at how art and literature enforce gender roles.

If you're a female student, there are many feminist organizations on campus including a women's resource center or union. If you're a male, don't be surprised if you are welcome to women's union events. Just make sure you ask for an invitation before showing up to show that you're not going just to meet girls. If you're a woman looking to meet other women in your own ethnic or religious group, there's a good chance you'll be able to find women's groups within larger organizations. You might find, for example, an African-American women's association, a Catholic women's prayer group, or an organization for Muslim women.

Sexual Orientation

A lot of college students don't really know who they are or what they like when they get to college. There's a lot of pressure in most high schools to fit in and be uniform. This means that a lot of gay teenagers have to "play straight" for years. Perhaps they're afraid to tell their family and friends or perhaps they're afraid to admit their sexual orientation to themselves.

In college, these restrictions disappear. There are many openly gay students and faculty on campus, which creates an instant community for students who are coming out. If you're a lesbian, gay, transgendered/transsexual, or bisexual student, seek out your school's LGBT association. Some large universities and liberal arts colleges also offer courses on gay and lesbian literature and history (often called Queer Studies). If you're questioning your sexual orientation, you'll always be welcome at any LGBT event on campus. You can also go there if you're heterosexual and "gay friendly"—straight but not narrow.

Experimenting with sexuality is common in college. Straight kids of the same sex may get together and gay kids may hook up with the opposite sex to see what it's like. People figure out who they are regardless of their experiences. You don't have to label yourself: just be sure to *be* yourself and only do what feels comfortable for you.

10 Things to Do When Friends Come Out to You

1. Don't assume they are hitting on you (don't flatter yourself!). Just like straight people aren't attracted to most people of the opposite sex, gay people aren't necessarily attracted to you just because you're the same sex, either.

2. Take it as a compliment. If someone is coming out to you, it means that she or he values your friendship and thinks you're trustworthy and understanding.

3. Don't act calmly and tell them they have your support and then run across the hall to gossip with excitement.

4. Ask them if it's OK if you "out" them in discussions with others. If they say no, respect their wishes.

"Identity would seem to be the garment with which one covers the nakedness of the self, in which case, it is best that the garment be loose, a little like the robes of the desert, through which one's nakedness can always be felt, and, sometimes, discerned."

James Baldwin

10
TIPS
For Coming Out

1. Don't be surprised if the person you're coming out to already knows, or has suspected, your sexual orientation.

2. It's better to come out to people privately than to blurt out your sexual identity to a large group.

3. Prepare yourself for questions about your sexuality.

4. Think about your motives for coming out to this person. Are you hoping that this person will better understand you? Are you afraid that they will hear about your sexual identity from another source? Do you want to let them know up front so you won't have to use ambiguous phrases like "my friend" or "my partner" or them and "they" instead of "him" or "her"?

5. Think about the moment ahead of time. For example, if you're coming out to a roommate, you might want to say, "I want to tell you upfront that I'm gay. I want to know if this is going to affect us as roommates."

6. Understand that your new friend or roommate may not accept you right away, if ever. If you feel that your living arrangement won't work out, go immediately to your RA and explain.

7. Don't be drunk or high when you come out, and don't come out to people who are drunk or high.

8. Give people time to process the information. Don't expect the "right" reaction right away.

9. Don't blurt out the news at odd times (e.g., while you're driving a car, in the middle of a silent candlelight vigil, while cliff climbing).

10. Remember that you have the right to leave a situation if you feel offended by someone's reaction.

5. Don't be judgmental. If you have strong beliefs that everyone should be straight, wait before discussing them. Tell your friend that you don't know what to say and that you need time to think things over. Respond only after careful thought.

6. If you're unsure what to say, learn about gay issues before you discuss the situation with your friend.

7. If your friend is transgendered or transsexual, ask which pronoun he or she prefers when being spoken to and about.

8. If your friend is transsexual, do not ask about his or her physiology or how he or she has sex.

9. Talk to your friends more frequently than you did before, to affirm that you really do care about them and accept them. Coming out can be scary.

10. If your friends are afraid of violence directed toward them now that they are out, don't dismiss that fear. Gay, lesbian, and transgendered people do experience discrimination. Instead, let them know that you are there for personal support.

Handling Independence

You have a right to shape your own identity, but remember: these rights come with responsibility. No matter how your sense of self changes over the years, part of personal growth is becoming responsible for yourself and communicating clearly with the people who are most important to you.

Responsibility

You're living on your own for the first time in your life. The habits that you develop now will follow you into your later adult years. Your mom isn't going to make your bed anymore. If you come from the kind of family where your

"My mother said to me, 'If you become a soldier, you'll be a general; if you become a monk, you'll end up as the Pope.' Instead, I became a painter and wound up as Picasso."

Pablo Picasso

parents made you do homework after dinner, those days are over. You never *have* to do homework again! Of course, you could fail out of college your first semester if you don't do your homework, but slacking off is an (unwise) option. In other words, success is *up to you.*

All of your discipline will have to come from within. Ask yourself: what kind of person am I? The type who blows off writing a paper to go to a couple of parties? The type who gossips about friends behind their backs? Not only do you have a responsibility to yourself, you have a responsibility to others and to the community at large.

Family

Whether you're a town away or ten states apart, your parents are going to see a lot less of you than they're used to, and they're probably going to be surprised at how rapidly you're changing. They only know the you that grew up in your hometown under *their* roof. Your parents might feel like they're losing you a little; this is a great time for you, but it will be a little hard on your folks.

Allow your parents to go through the feelings of loss that come with having their child leave for school. Their sadness may come out in weird ways. They may get mad or weepy, or they may call you a know-it-all for arguing every point you learned in your Intro to Sociology course. If you ever feel like your family issues are getting to be a bit much, head to your school's counseling or mental health center for guidance.

Old Friendships

"Depth of friendship does not depend on length of acquaintance."

Rabindranath Tagore

What about your best high school buddy? Is he truly your best friend because you have a deep emotional bond and lots in common? Or are you so close because you live in the same town, share the same experiences, and gossip about the same people? Remember, unless your friends are going to the same college, they're not going to know the ins and outs of your daily life anymore. As a result, you might not feel as close to them.

Will your old friends accept the fact that you want to experiment with religion? If they aren't in college themselves, will they respect that you may be studying for hours at a time and unable to call them back to chat on the phone? If you decide that you're done with being preppy and it's time for a blue Mohawk, will they still be your pals? If the answer is *yes* to all of these questions, then you have true friends on your hands, and you should cherish those friendships and keep in touch. But if your high school buddies were merely "friends of convenience," you'll find out fast. If this is the case, don't be afraid to move on.

Your College Town

The environment that surrounds your college is most likely to affect you when it is very different then your hometown. If you are currently living in Murfreesboro, Arkansas, and you're about to start at New York University in downtown Manhattan, boy, are you in for a change of scenery. Likewise, if you've lived in Los Angeles, you're going to have culture shock if you're attending the University of Iowa or a small liberal arts college in Vermont.

Your new town adds to an aspect of your identity. You can choose to either identify with the town and become a citizen, or to have disdain for the town and bash it every time someone mentions it. Believe us, you're better off embracing the town, because even if you don't love it while you're there, you're going to be very nostalgic about it when you're gone.

Community Service

Community service is a great way to become part of your new town and discover yourself as an individual. Locate political organizations, businesses, hospitals, charities, or houses of worship that have a purpose that suits your ideals. If working with children interests you, check to see if there's a children's hospital where you can volunteer. If you'd like to be a political activist, find the civic organizations in your new area. An internship at a local business can give you valuable career training and help you under-stand the social codes of your new setting. But remember, if you need to set up a job or internship right away, make sure to get the ball rolling as soon as you settle into your new life at college.

The Bottom Line

In your first year of college, you'll transform from wide-eyed kid into adult faster than you can say "final exam." Be prepared for rapid growth, but don't worry about finding that one perfect permanent identity right away. Your identity will change along with your education and life experiences. But you'll find that everyone else you meet in college will be going through changes too. You've come this far. Now open yourself to some new ideas and let your best judgment be your guide.

10
SUMMER

"I was both happy and sad that my first year was over. Happy that classes were done, but sad that I was moving away from my new friends for the summer. I was also kind of freaked out that I was moving back in with my folks. I didn't know what to expect."

Bridget G.
University of Kansas

At the end of your first year, you will face a big decision: where to go? Do you move back in with Mom and Dad, or do you stick around campus? Most colleges won't let you hang out in the dorm for the summer. Unless you're taking summer classes, you'll have to clear out as soon as finals week is over.

You'll also be faced with starting to think about what to major in and whether you'll return to the same school next fall. Most of you are reading this book before your first year of college has started, so it might seem like we're jumping the gun here. But it's important to plan ahead: if you find yourself having to make a quick decision, you will want to have already considered all your options.

Staying Put

Staying put in the dorms means doing the summer school thing; if you're not enrolled in classes, the school won't let you stay in a dorm room. Staying put in your college town means finding off-campus housing and getting a summer job.

Some schools offer special summer programs that combine classes, internships, and work-study. These programs will look great on your résumé when you graduate, so they're definitely worth checking out.

Back with the 'Rents

Moving back in with your parents for the summer after the freedom of college life can be challenging. You're suddenly faced with all the old rules. You're also going to have to deal with someone prying into your life, asking where you're going and whom you're going with.

It will be important to find a way to express how you've changed and matured without getting into a fight over it. Your parents may still think of you as the kid you were when you left for college, so your job is to project a different image—that of the responsible adult.

Summer Classes

If you end up sticking around campus for the summer, you can get a jump-start on your sophomore year by taking summer classes.

10 Reasons to Opt for Summer Classes

1. **Bring up your GPA.** If your grades were less than sparkling during the year, taking one or two classes in the summer can help bring up your GPA. Since you'll be taking fewer classes, you can really focus on the subject at hand.

2. **Learn from chilled-out profs.** Summer classes aren't easier, but professors tend to be more lenient in the summer.

3. **Get to know your profs.** Getting to know your professors can be difficult during the school year when you're competing for their attention with hundreds of other students. Over the summer, you'll have an opportunity to build a one-on-one relationship.

4. **Live on your own.** You won't have to move back in with your parents for the summer, a big relief for some students.

5. **Avoid getting a job.** If the prospect of a minimum-wage job back at home gives you nightmares, taking a class will keep you busy and will keep your parents off your case for not working over the summer.

6. **Pay less for school.** Many colleges charge lower tuition for summer classes.

7. **Meet new people.** There aren't a ton of people on campus during the summer, but those that stick around definitely find one another.

High School Chums

You'll be surprised by the number of high school friends you'll hang out with over the summer—surprised by how low that number is. Your old pals will have made new friends or might not come home for the summer. Like you, they will have changed a lot during their first year at college, and that will change your relationships.

TIPS

For Getting Along with Your Parents

1. **Pitch in.** We know you're not used to being told to do household tasks anymore, but if the rest of the family has to do chores, so do you.

2. **Keep quiet.** Your folks might not be used to the new hours you keep, so be quiet when you're up making a sandwich at four in the morning.

3. **Negotiate rules.** If your folks try to maintain old rules from your high school days, explain that you've matured and that you'd appreciate a little wiggle room.

4. **Respect rules.** Once you've decided on the house rules for the summer, don't break them.

5. **Know where you stand.** Ask your parents what they expect from you now that you're back. This will give them the opportunity to think about how they have approached you in the past and how they should approach you now.

6. **Be considerate.** If you're an adult, prove it. Clean up after yourself, or cook a meal for your family.

7. **Put yourself in their shoes.** Try to see every situation from your parents' perspective. Maybe they're not trying to treat you like a child by asking you to be home at 2 A.M. Maybe they just can't sleep until you get home because they worry about you.

8. **Stay cool.** If you've done something drastic, like pierced something, gotten a tattoo, or dyed your hair blue, expect some flak over it. Take it in stride.

9. **Be present.** You might miss school a lot, but if you mention that at the dinner table every night, you're bound to cause some hurt feelings.

10. **Be patient.** Remember, this too shall pass. Summer is short: you'll be back at college soon enough.

8. **Meet the locals.** Local residents (also known as *townies*) are generally much friendlier and easier to meet over the summer. In small towns, it's the one time of the year when they actually outnumber the students.

9. **Take advantage of the town.** Because summer is a slow time for most college towns, cultural venues and restaurants have special offers.

10. **Fulfill requirements.** If you've settled on a major, get some of those requirements out of the way over the summer so you can focus on the classes you really want to take during sophomore year.

Repeating a Class

Summer is a good time to retake any classes you failed. When you retake a class, the new grade doesn't necessarily replace the old grade. While the passing grade will count toward your graduation credit, both grades are factored into your cumulative GPA. So don't be cavalier about your regular semester classes thinking that you'll just make them up in the summer if necessary.

Summer Jobs

Your college's career center will hold a summer job fair during the spring term to help students find a summer job. Those jobs are often geared toward a certain career and require more discipline than you might want for your first summer. Summer jobs for first-year students don't have to be résumé builders. You can choose something fun that will earn you extra cash.

If you are a pre-professional student (medical, dental, law, business, etc.), the summer after your first year is your last opportunity to goof off. After sophomore year you'll probably be expected to get a part-time or full-time summer job related to your prospective field.

Summer School at Home

If you absolutely have to (or want to) go back home, you can take classes at a local college. A community college is your best bet, since it will be far less expensive. Call your school's registrar to make sure that the classes you take during the summer will transfer.

10

SUMMER JOBS
For First Years

Internships

An internship is a professional job that earns you college credit and, in many cases, money. If you opt for a summer internship, you'll work long hours, but you'll gain valuable résumé-building experience. If you want to enter a field that requires hands-on experience, such as working in a television newsroom, a hospital, or a publishing house, an internship is an ideal way to get your foot in the door. The career center will have summer internship listings at the beginning of the spring semester.

During your internship, you'll get to meet people in your prospective field who can help you get a job after college. Be nice and helpful to *everyone* at the company where you intern. The mailroom girl or the copy boy could get promoted in the next few years and wind up being your boss someday.

Transferring

There are many reasons why students transfer after their first year. Perhaps they aren't happy with their college and they want to find a better fit. Perhaps their family circumstances have changed and they need to move closer to home. Whatever the case, if you want to transfer to another college you'll have to go through the whole process of applying to schools all over again. That means new application essays, new teacher recommendations, and new interviews. However, it could be well worth it.

10 Reasons Why You Might Transfer

1. You're moving from a two-year school to a four-year school: if you started out at a two-year institution, you'll have to transfer to earn an BA or BS.

2. You're doing poorly academically: perhaps you *have* to leave because you're on academic suspension or you've failed a bunch of classes.

3. The classes aren't challenging enough: perhaps you're ready for a more rigorous academic workout. You'll find it's a lot easier to get into some of those upper-ranked schools when you transfer.

4. The social scene isn't your thing: not everyone is suited for a party college or an egghead school.

10

Transferring Tips

1   Make sure you have all of your transcripts in order. Make photocopies and keep records of all paperwork.

2   Don't slack off during those last few months before you transfer. There's a tendency to let academics slide when you're on your way out, but keep in mind that your undergrad grades are important no matter where you are.

3   When you arrive at the new school, attend transfer orientation. We know, you just did first-year orientation, but you'll need to learn the lay of the land at your new school.

4   Find other transfer students. Unless you're transferring to a very small school, realize that you're not alone. You'll meet a lot of other people who have transferred too.

5   Live on campus, even if you don't have to. If you're coming in as a sophomore you may not have to live on campus, but it's a good idea anyway. You'll meet more people and become part of the university scene more easily than if you lived off campus.

6   Go to your academic counselor as soon as possible. You'll want to go over your transcript and choose your classes wisely based on potential academic weak spots.

7   Join clubs or go to on-campus activities. The sooner you make new friends, the happier you'll be.

8   Go with the flow in class. Even if you're required to repeat a requirement at your new school, you'll still be introduced to new ideas and ways of thinking. Always be open-minded in class.

9   Give some thought to the money you'll need. Is your new college town more expensive? Plan on getting a job if necessary. Because you're a sophomore, you may have a leg up on the first-year students.

10 If you transfer midyear, stick around over the summer. Students who transfer in January are just getting used to their new surroundings by the time summer rolls around. By staying on campus for three extra months, you'll feel much more at home when the new school year starts.

5. Your school doesn't offer enough courses in the disciplines you're interested in, or it doesn't offer the major you think you want to shoot for. Don't choose a major that doesn't interest you just because doing so is easier than applying to a new school.

6. School is too expensive: even with financial aid and a job, a private school might be too much of burden. If that's the case, transferring to a state school is your best bet.

7. The weather is killing you: if you're a beach bum at heart, going to a college in Buffalo, New York, probably wasn't the best idea. If you're a snowboarder who tried a school in South Florida, then pack it up and move out if you're miserable. But we recommend waiting another year and giving it the old "college try." Perhaps you'll learn to love the snow.

8. Your health is suffering: if you have severe asthma and you're enrolled at UCLA, leaving for a less smoggy locale would be a smart move.

9. You have to move back home: many students transfer because of a family emergency or other family issues.

10. You're following a sweetheart: hey, who are we to interfere with true love? But think about what you're doing. How long have you known your honey? Long enough to leave a college you spent so much time getting into? Is this a relationship that's definitely going somewhere in the long term? See if you can wait another year to move to make sure that the relationship will last.

Choosing a Major

While most colleges require you to choose a major at the end of your sopho-more year, you should start thinking about your academic future now. After a year of college classes, you'll probably have a pretty good idea of what direction you want to go in.

Take a look at your transcripts and see what classes you excelled in. If you want to be a doctor, but you can't pass chemistry and math, you may want to rethink your goals. Your first two years of college should be geared toward figuring out your academic strengths and weaknesses. Taking your personal profile into account will help you to choose a major.

Studying Abroad

Your school should have dozens of study-abroad opportunities. Scholarships and grants are available for study-abroad programs, so do your homework if you can't afford to pay for one on your own. Generally, study-abroad programs require you to take a class in the history and culture of the country you're studying in, as well as a language course.

The Bottom Line

The bottom line is this: whatever you do, have a plan. Even if that plan is simply to go back home and get a job in a coffee shop, be prepared for all the challenges that come with moving back in with your parents. If you plan on summer classes, get your head set for studying, not summer vacation. If you plan to study abroad, make a packing list and get prepared for the experience of a lifetime. Whatever you choose, know that the summer is fleeting, and in a couple of months you'll be back at school, that much older and that much wiser.

Surviving the summer and the years ahead isn't much different than surviving your first year of college. Being successful in life means being able to adapt to new situations. If you come prepared for every challenge, you will get the most out of your experiences and you will never stop learning.

Good luck!

ACKNOWLEDGMENTS

The author would like to thank Ziki Dekel, the wonderful editor on this book; Laurie Barnett, the editorial director, for making it possible; and everyone who helped me along the way.